① login

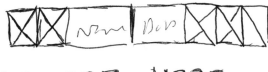

(handwritten notes: circled ①; circled ② log in; boxed "new Dev"; "Agent - 855-937-4325"; "member - 866-541-7348"; "Advocacy")

Agent - 855 - 937 - 4325
member - 866 - 541 - 7348
Advocacy

Insurance Agency Optimization

A Proven Step-by-Step Guide to Market Domination

(handwritten: Adroit Health; 3 visits)

Scott Grates

(handwritten: August 1, 2019)

Insurance Agency Optimization

Independently Published
Copyright © 2019, Scott Grates

Published in the United States of America

181206-01251-4

ISBN: 9781099492310

For more information on 90-Minute Books including finding out how you
can publish your own book, visit 90minutebooks.com or call (863) 318-0464

Here's What's Inside...

Introduction

The goal of this book is to give you a high level overview on being a productive agent as well as, proven strategies on running a super successful insurance agency. It's about getting you away from the old way of doing things, which are typically broken and backward. We will also help you put some parameters around your work and life balance; to improve your health and happiness, which ultimately leads us to better results at the agency.

The primary goal of this book is to let agents know, "you're not alone; you're not on an island." I've lived your life for the past 10 years. I've had a high level of success in a market that economically struggles. It's a small rural market, and we've been recognized as one of the top agencies nationally for a decade now. We don't do anything magical. There's no secret formula.

We do *simple things better* and more consistently. We focus on every single customer interaction as an opportunity to learn more about them, to help them, and ultimately deliver on our promise to always keep the customer first.

There is no difference between "sales" and "service." We focus on conversations, regardless how they start. More conversations create more opportunities. The depth of those conversations will determine the height of your agency's success. People choose to do business with, people they KNOW, LIKE and TRUST. Insurance Agency Optimization is all about creating a book of business field with people who KNOW, LIKE and TRUST you!

I also want you to realize there is a true "win-win" scenario with this insurance agency opportunity when it comes to work/life balance. I guess it's a win-win-win-win when you break it all down.

You can have the time you want, to live the life you want to live. Professionally, you can help your customers in more ways than ever by doing the right thing for the right person at the right moment. You can give back to the community you serve through volunteering your time and your money. You can help those you employ as insurance producers to become better people, bigger producers and build their own career. When done properly, you can check every box and win every area, personally, professionally, as a coach, as a trainer, as a mentor, as a community leader, and feel proud about what you do and leave a legacy behind that lasts long after you are gone.

My hope for you, the reader, is to gain massive value out of this book, take away one, two, or three key components which you can implement immediately. The strategies and steps I share in this book are proven to work and will grow your agency, regardless of market.

Everything I share will be simple, but none of it will be easy. After you finish reading this book my desire is you and your team will feel inspired to immediately take action; by, implementing these proven systems and strategies, so you can quickly cash in on all the positive impacts available to you in life and at your agency.

Chapter 1:
You Never Planned on Being an Insurance Agent

I could not wait to begin my career as a sports reporter. It was 1999, I'd just graduated from college with a journalism degree and I was ready to make a name for myself in the newspaper industry. However, my first career lesson came in the field of mathematics when I was offered a job at the local newspaper for $7 an hour. Unfortunately, I was loaded with debt from my college years, and I quickly realized I could not pay my bills earning $7 an hour. One Sunday I saw an ad in the paper for a job selling furniture, with the promise of making $35,000 a year. I asked myself, "How hard can that be?" I went, I interviewed, I got the job, and I soon found out how hard it was. Very hard, as it turned out!

Retail, was my baptism by fire into the world of sales. I was working nights, weekends, holidays, and to make things even worse, it was 100% on commission. There I was, in my polished shoes and cheap suit, trying to sell sofas to people who were always, "just looking."

After my now-wife graduated from college, we moved from New York to Virginia where I jumped into the field of Real Estate. After five extremely successful years and the birth of our first child, we decided to raise our family back home. With much lower home values in Central New York I did not see Real Estate in my future, so I made the move into the mortgage industry. Within two years I had become recognized as one of the top producers in the country, but in 2008, the financial crisis hit and the bank I was working for closed shop; 6,500 jobs were gone overnight, including mine.

I asked myself, "Now what?" I was at a crossroads; I had tremendous success as a salesperson. Every place I worked, I was ranked in the top five percent nationally. I was earning money, trips and I had received high-quality sales training from some of the best mentors and leaders in the field.

I learned the psychology of sales, how to create emotion for my prospects around my products. I learned how to follow a sales process, I learned there had to be a logical order to the process, and that your words matter. I also realized success does not happen overnight, without constantly practicing and leaving your comfort zone, improvement can never be made.

There I was, 31 years old; I had 10 years of tremendous success in sales, but grew tired of the month-to-month grind. I was sick of being a hero on July 31st and back to a zero on August first. I had a journalism degree which I never used and a resume loaded with success and experience from an industry I was burned out on. I had a wife and two children at the time who were counting on me to pay the bills. What did I do? I became an insurance agent.

It's funny, I do seminars all over the country and I always ask the insurance agents "how many of you dreamt of being an insurance agent when you were a kid, raise your hand." No one ever raises their hand! None of us ever wanted to get here. I then ask, "Why did we get into the field of insurance?"

My reasons for getting into this business were probably some of the same basic reasons you initially had. I thought to myself, "Well, everyone needs insurance, and it provides residual income, so how hard can it be to get a bunch of people to allow me to write their auto policies?" Very Hard! It turned out.

The Difficult Reality of Insurance Sales

The concepts around selling insurance are simple, but consistently producing at a high level is not easy. What I didn't know when I began was not only would it be extremely difficult to write auto, home, life and health policies. Then, it was even harder to get people to stay with you once you did write their policies. The people who do stay require a high level of service month after month.

As an insurance agency owner, nobody told me how difficult it would be to recruit, train, hire, inspire, continuously motivate and educate employees. Even worse, nobody told me when and how to fire the bad ones. No one told me how to be an HR manager or write a handbook. Nobody ever told me I would have to figure out marketing, advertising, budgeting, bookkeeping, taxes, law changes, computer system updates, underwriting changes, how to manage claims, how to deal with billing issues, cultivate relationships with referral sources.

But wait we're not finished. Nobody told me I'd be taking calls seven days a week or answering questions at cookouts and birthday parties or that I'd have to move money from lines of credit or max out credit cards to make certain payrolls. Nobody told me I'd lose sleep worrying about something I forgot to do or how we'll hit our goals.

I wanted to be an insurance agent because I thought it would be easy to write a bunch of auto policies. After all, everybody needs insurance, but nobody told me how hard this gig really is. There I sat. I was left alone to figure it all out after I started. Day one, I had no customers and no clue how to run an insurance agency. I didn't even know who to ask for help. What did I do? I started cheating off other people's papers.

What if You're Cheating Off the Wrong Paper?

Ever make a copy of a copy? It's not as clean as the original, right? What I discovered in the insurance industry is newbies turn to veteran agents for knowledge, information, systems, and processes. When the vets share how they've done things, newbies take it as gospel. However, there are two problems with this.

First, you can't put square pegs in round holes, and everybody's different. Teams are different, premiums are different, regulations are different, the markets we serve are different, and everybody has a different style. What works for one person doesn't always work for another.

The second problem was some of the veteran agents weren't giving the best advice. They were passing along things they were told is "the truth" but as it turned out much of it was the same old backwards way of doing business. They shared broken mindsets such as, "people only buy on the rate, and people have no money for life and health policies, if you quote more, you'll sell more, or, if you spend more on marketing, you'll increase revenue." They treated all team members the same and essentially just wanted to plug me into an already broken system. The insurance industry was rapidly changing, I knew if I was going to find the level of success I desired, I couldn't do business the same way others before me had.

We operate in a highly competitive, highly commoditized industry. If you are going to stand out and be noticed when everybody is running to the left, you need to start sprinting to the right. When you only do what those before you did, you'll limit your potential to only getting what they got. Any time new information is sent your way, you must use a sifter, so to speak, to process what works best for you.

Think of yourself as a prospector during the 1800s gold rush. You put all the information you get into your sifter, shake it, and then you keep the gold and throw away the dirt. Don't be the person who does everything a certain way because that's the way it's always been done or because that's the way somebody else did it before you. Instead, you have only to keep the golden ideas, melt those down, and mold them to fit the shape and style of your agency.

Does the Magic Formula for Success Exist?

The biggest breakthrough you'll ever have in your career is the day you realize the breakthrough concept does not exist. There is no magic formula or silver bullet or shortcut to success. Instead, you have to master the mundane and consistently execute on winning each moment of your day. To do this, you must have a plan in place to win your day along with a long-term vision of where these small daily wins will eventually lead you.

Too many people chase rainbows, butterflies, and unicorns when it comes to their quest for success. They travel all over the country and spend thousands of dollars on the latest and greatest seminar or training *du jour*. They convince themselves, as soon as they know what she does, or they say what he says, they will experience the same levels of success.

Once you stop searching for this winning lottery ticket and wholeheartedly believe there are no shortcuts to success, it's then and only then you'll put yourself on the right path towards the success you so desperately seek.

Common Denominators

There are indisputable common denominators to success that the happiest, healthiest, most productive people on our planet have focused on since the beginning of time. Race, religion, color, creed, gender, financial status, geographic location, or age, do not matter. When you focus your time and energy on following simple daily disciplines, your results will improve in every facet of your life.

14 Key Areas

There are 14 key areas I focus on each day so I can WIN EVERY DAY. These key areas are available to our MASTERMIND GROUP in their Toolbox found and detailed on our website www.agencyoptimization.com.

If you have not taken the time to review all of the agency changing benefits available to our MASTERMIND members yet, you should! Hop over there before starting Chapter 2 (which is only a page away).

A couple examples of these "WIN EVERY DAY" key areas would be <u>establishing a morning routine</u>. You must make a choice to own certain parts of your day, and the morning is the easiest part for most, if you need an extra 30 minutes in your day, you set your alarm for 30 minutes earlier. A winning morning routine will create momentum and result in you winning your day.

You have to <u>set daily goals</u>. If you are doing something in your head, it's a dream, but once you write it down on paper, it becomes a goal. There's power in writing goals on paper. Once you write them in your personal playbook each day, you've now made a commitment to yourself and your chances of achieving them increase significantly.

<u>Create an essential list.</u> This list contains only the essential, must-do activities for each day. You create your essential list the night before. Write down three things you must get done the following day, put them in order of priority, and then tomorrow, the very first thing you do is attack that list with laser-like focus starting with whatever is number one. Once priority one is completed, you can then move on to number two.

These were just a few examples of my 14 key areas, the other eleven can be found at our website at **www.positiveimpactclub.com**. It's under the (PIC Shop tab) "Win Every Day."

Do You Already Have the Ingredients?

Too many people believe it requires a massive change to realize massive results. The truth is you are already on the right track and probably only need to make a few small changes in order to fine-tune your agency. When you try to do too much at one time, you end up doing nothing. *It's like watching* a person carrying seven items. He drops one, tries to pick it up, and then drops three more. The Pareto principle tells us that 80% of results come from 20% of our efforts.

Simply focus on improving one aspect of your business at a time and don't try to do everything all at once.

Chapter 2:
What Agency Optimization is and Why it Works

You must be able to close what I refer to as the *knowledge-action gap*. There's an old cliché that knowledge is power, but it's not true. Knowledge without action is useless. The Agents who take action on what they learn are those who realize the highest levels of success.

Within the insurance industry I believe there is a 90/10 rule when it comes to success; which is 90% of people start things, but only 10% finish. 90% of those who start this book will never finish it. The most successful people (the 10%), are finishers. Starting is easy. Successful people are obsessed with finishing.

I believe in the insurance industry, 90% of agents are either coasting or endlessly searching for solutions while 10% have systems, processes, and word tracks that fit the style of their agency. Those 10% focus on fine-tuning things. They practice, consistently execute on daily success disciplines and they follow the proven sales process they have in place.

Time Management

When you try to be all things to all people all the time, you turn yourself into a hamster on a wheel. You're always running 1,000 miles an hour but never getting anywhere. Busy is not better, so stop convincing yourself you don't have time and you're always too busy. That 90% group of agents who can't figure this gig out is filled with people who are busy but not productive.

The greatest conversation I ever had with a mentor insurance agent is when I called him and said, "Hey, Ron, I never have time to get anything done." He paused, and fired back to me a million-dollar question, one that echoed in my head for all the years that followed. He said, "Scott, what do you do with your time all day? Tell me what a typical day looks like for you at the agency. I want to know everything you're doing from the minute you walk through the door."

Immediately, I was stumped. I was silent. My mind was rushing in 10 different directions, but I was embarrassed to share everything that I was thinking. I thought about things like email, reading reports, answering phones, scanning documents, chatting with customers who stopped in, following up on underwriting and claims activities. It was then I realized how REACTIVE I was being.

I was allowing outside factors to dictate my actions. It was then I realized I had no plan and the bulk of what I was doing each day wasn't productive. It wasn't moving me closer to my goals, and it wasn't making me happy. It was then I realized I needed to create *my essential list*. My big Ah Ha moment was when I realized everything that wasn't on that list needed to be delegated.

I realized I was living a lie. I was telling myself I was the CEO of my own agency, but I was working as an entry-level service rep. I was telling myself I was too busy, but the reality was I wasn't organized, productive, or efficient with my time.

Let's go back to the essential list. Before you leave the office each day, you must write down your top three priorities for tomorrow. Once you have those three priorities, put them in order, one, two, and three.

When you get to the office the next day, with laser-like focus, make sure you get through number one. You don't move on to number two until you get number one done.

In my agency, I use what I refer to as the "Triple D approach." It stands for: do, delegate, or destroy. (You can use "decline" if you don't like as much destruction in your life.) What this means is, for anything that comes across your desk, you have three options. You can do it and do it immediately, you can delegate it to somebody else, or you can destroy it or decline it by saying no. What you cannot do is say yes to anything that's not on your essential list and you cannot allow essential activities to be moved to the back burner.

Pushing Out of Your Comfort Zone

Just on the other side of fear lies some of the most exciting, happy, gratifying moments of your life. When you allow fear to hijack you and control your actions or create inactions, you can never reach your full potential. In order to reach your maximum potential you must start doing more of the things which make you the most uncomfortable. For a person to succeed in the insurance world, it's crucial they understand how the primitive brain works and that within our skulls is outdated equipment.

The brain was programmed using software from 2,000 years ago. Its two main goals each day are to one, keep you safe, and two, keep you running efficiently. Unfortunately, when it comes to modern-day business, our brains work against us. It's crucial we realize this, so we can recognize when it happens and then respond accordingly.

At first, this feels unnatural and uncomfortable because you'll be defying your own head. Your brain will be telling you to run away, but instead, you're going to run towards your fears. Keep in mind, thousands of years ago, humans lived in caves, roamed the earth with wild animals, and had to find their own food. It was crucial for our brains to tell us to run when there was a saber tooth tiger nearby or to protect us from eating poisonous berries.

Fortunately, in today's world, things are a bit less wild. However, our primitive brain still sends us signals to run when it senses danger. At the agency, when you ask for a sale and get an objection, your heart speeds up, your breathing becomes shorter, and you feel a certain level of fear. Your brain is telling you to get out of the situation, and 90% of producers listen.

However, the most successful people in the industry receive the "run-away" message from their brain, and use it as a prompt to do the opposite. Slow down, calm down, take a deep breath, and overcome that objection.

The good news is, with every fear-based situation we face at our agencies, if we go against our brain's initial response, there's a very low probability that it will lead to our death. When you actually break down the things you fear the most at the agency, they aren't that scary at all. Come to think of it, I have never seen a saber tooth tiger at the office!

Your brain's second goal is to run efficiently. It tells you to pick the low hanging fruit, travel down the road of least resistance. When given an option of what's easiest versus difficult, your brain will always tell you to take the easy way. Again, those in the 90% listen while the other 10% realize the only way to improve and succeed is to become comfortable with being uncomfortable. Then your actions will work accordingly.

When a customer asks you for a quote on their auto, you can take the path of least resistance by reading the questions, inserting their answers and spit out a quote. Or, you can take the time to have a conversation, ask deeper questions, get to know your prospect, and offer them solutions for all of their needs. When a customer walks into the agency to make a payment, you can take the payment and let them leave. Or, you can take the time to get to know them, schedule a review appointment, and ask them who insures their paycheck or their legacy.

When you write new business for a customer, you can include a flyer offering a $10 gift card in exchange for the names of their friends and family. Or, you can spend a few minutes explaining how important referrals are to your livelihood, why you are asking for them and how you are the best person to protect their friends and family.

The Rock Star Referral System is explained in Chapter 9. It is also featured as "Must Win Area #16" of the 20 training videos available to our MASTERMIND members. The corresponding documents are in the Toolbox. This system yields my agency over 1,000 referrals each year and generates over six figure profits annually

Your OBLIGATION as an Insurance Producer

So many insurance producers focus too much time and energy on production numbers. I want to challenge you to stop focusing on numbers and start focusing on the obligation you have and the impact you can make as a licensed insurance producer. I want you to start asking the questions that need to be asked even if you're afraid of coming across as "salesie."

I want you to stop comparing yourself to other insurance producers and start focusing on what the person in front of you needs the most. No more, "I can't do what she does." No more, "I'm not as good as he is." I'm calling BS because we all have the same tools. We all have the same opportunity to talk to people, but the problem is we all don't do it.

Why not? Many insurance producers lack the self-confidence and practice. Here's the thing, if you truly love what you do, and you know the people you interact with need what you have and you know your actions will make a difference to them and their families; and, you know you can have a long-lasting positive impact long after you're gone, then you have an obligation to share this knowledge and passion you possess with every single person you interact with.

If you truly believe in your products and yourself, you have an obligation to share that with everybody. We share, influence and recommend all sorts of useless stuff to people every day: a movie we liked, a song we enjoy, a restaurant we can't get enough of. Every single day, you encourage and inspire people to take action on things, but you don't label it as selling. Stop thinking you are bothering people or bugging people when you are inspiring them and encouraging them to take action on the things that matter most.

As humans, we all want freedom and options. People fear the unknown, which often blocks them from taking action on something they don't understand. However, it's the customer's fear that stops them and, ultimately, penalizes them when the unknown and the unthinkable does happen.

Sure. If we all lived in a perfect little bubble where we're born, instantly happy and healthy and we never get sick and never fail, and nobody cried or died, then there would be no need for insurance producers. But guess what? The world needs more insurance producers. The world needs more quality insurance producers, people who aren't scared to have more needs-based, value-based conversations.

If customers were forced to be honest with you, they would tell you they don't want five seconds of life to change their "everything" forever. They don't want to take that dreaded call or get that unthinkable diagnosis or be involved in an accident or experience a fire. What they do want to do is maintain their normal life. They don't want change. They fear change, but the problem is they don't know how to protect their normal life properly.

They don't know what they need, how much they need, or even where to get what they need, but what they need is right in front of them. They need someone they can trust, someone who's honest and sincere who will do what's in their best interest, someone who's going to put their needs first, someone who's willing to ask the right questions, listen to those answers, and care.

They need someone who's willing to give a damn when they need that person the most.

They need you, but you are worried about coming across as "salesie." Please stop feeling that way because you have an obligation as an insurance producer to protect the person right in front of you, from themselves.

Their fear of change is preventing them from protecting against what they fear the most, which is a life-altering change. You can't be "their person" until you start believing you ARE the BEST person to protect them. In fact, it's your obligation to believe it.

Chapter 3:
Health and Happiness Lead to Success, Not the Other Way Around

Too many people have a backward mindset when it comes to happiness and success. They think that once they're successful, then they will be happy. However, the reality is it's those who are healthy and happy first who ultimately find the highest levels of success. When your brain is in a positive state, and your body is properly fueled, you have more energy, discover more opportunities, and produce at a higher level than those who are in a negative mindset and lethargic at the agency.

Think of yourself as an elite athlete. Your "kickoff" or your "opening tip" is at 9:00 AM. It's when your game starts, but it shouldn't be when your daily preparation begins.

A professional basketball player would never take his first shot of the day during the game. They practice ahead of time. They have an essential list of items that are an important part of their preparation before a game like proper hydration and diet, meditation, stretching, positive journaling and game planning. They have a goal to win, take some practice shots and mentally prepare. They visualize themselves succeeding. Athletes warm themselves up and prepare for success; you need a morning routine so you can do the same thing when your day starts at 9:00 AM.

Tips and Tricks

The world sends us a disproportionate amount of negative to positive messages. Within an insurance agency, you can take that negative ratio and multiply it by 10. Nobody ever calls your insurance agency to thank you for taking their money each month. They don't compliment you on how comfortable they feel with the level of protection you've provided for the possible future date when something bad *might* happen.

No. Instead, they call the agency because they're upset about a rate increase, not happy with a claim, they're having a billing issue, or they're confused about their coverages. Some are cordial and polite, but most aren't. That's on the service end.

On the sales end of business, you're calling people all day long who don't want to talk to you. They don't understand how you can help. They don't believe they need your products. They blow you off for appointments. They tell you they went with somebody else, or they stayed where they were. It's crucial that you stay in a positive mindset within this negative environment. You cannot allow a bad call to carry over to the next.

You must believe the next person you talk to will become your biggest and best customer ever. Within the first 15 seconds of a conversation, a person has already decided if they like you or not. If you allow your negative emotions from the previous call to carry over to the next, it will cause you to ruin what could potentially be your best opportunity of the day.

Here are some success points on how to keep a positive mindset.

- Remove yourself from the situation, literally. Get up, take a walk. You shouldn't be chained to your desk.
- Use the buddy system. Pick somebody you can vent to for 30 seconds or less and then agree that it's over. Then you do the same for that person.
- Combat breathing where you breathe in for five seconds, hold your breath for five seconds and exhale for five seconds. Do that a few times in a row.

- Don't take things personally. Don't accept the other person's anger as your own.
- Keep your main thing the main thing.
  - Post pictures of family or friends at your desk.
  - Keep your goals and your essential list at your desk.
  - Write the names of your favorite customers down and post them at your desk.

Then use them to refocus on why you do what you do with the people who matter the most and keep some of your happiest moment's right in front of you.

Dr. Kevin Elko coined the phrase, "So what? Now what?" Regardless of what happens, so what? The important question then becomes, "Now what?" Yes, negative things and undesirable outcomes will happen all day long. So what? Now, what are you going to do about it? I haven't personally seen the goals or compensation plans for everybody who's reading this book, but I guarantee there's no reward for the number of pity parties you throw for yourself each day. You cannot allow these negative moments to compound and carry over to the rest of your day.

Routines and Habits

In my established morning routine, the hour of the day that I can control is that first hour. Make a commitment to kill your snooze button. You have hundreds of decisions to make every single day. Don't allow your first decision to be: go back to sleep. Let your competition sleep in (and then complain they never have time to get anything done).

My morning routine consists of getting up, stretching, hydrating, meditating, positive journaling, writing goals for the day, learning something new and eating a healthy breakfast. I accomplish all of that in the first 30 to 45 minutes of my morning while my house is still quiet. This puts me in the best possible mindset and puts me on a path for success to win my day.

People don't plan to fail; they fail to plan.

The reason 90% of the agents in this industry can't crack into that top 10% is they don't have a plan on how to win each moment and, ultimately, win every day. They wander through each day aimlessly, and then when critical situations arise, or an opportunity presents itself, they make a poor decision and never see the opportunity because they weren't properly prepared.

In order to give myself a head start over the competition I execute on a strict evening routine. My evening routine is designed to limit the number of decisions I have to make the following day. I start by laying out my clothes that I'm going to exercise and picking out the clothes I'm going to wear to the office the following day. I prep the next day's breakfast and lunch. I create and prioritize the following day's essential list. I reflect on the day that happened. I score myself on the "win every day checklist" to make sure I completed a majority of my daily disciplines. I also make sure I do not eat food after 7:00 PM. I drink soothing decaf tea only, and I shut down electronics at least 30 minutes prior to sleep.

With proper preparation during your evening routine, you can start your following day five steps ahead of the rest of the world, and your production results at the agency will reflect that.

Sitting is the New Smoking

The human body was not created to sit. Unfortunately, our job as insurance agents has us sitting way more than we should. There are the obvious health risks associated with sitting for extended periods of time, such as bad back and neck pain. Recently, medical studies have shown that keeping your body in a seated position for the bulk of your day can also lead to high blood pressure, diabetes, and even death.

A study from Columbia University shows people who sit for 13 hours or more each day have twice the chance of dying versus those who sit for 11 hours. Standing for two additional hours each day will significantly improve your overall health. Regarding how long you should be sitting at one time, the same study shows, people who sat for 30 minutes or longer had a 55% greater chance of illness versus those who got up and moved before hitting that 30-minute mark.

Remember, your health and happiness will increase your productivity at the agency. Make it a point to get up every 20 minutes or so to stretch, walk, hydrate. Regular movement will curb your feelings of anxiety and stress. When you get up and increase your heart rate and get your blood pumping faster, your body then releases serotonin, which helps improve your state of mind, making stresses at work easier to handle and will keep your mindset more positive.

Coffee is for Closers

Another trap we fall into in the insurance world is our consumption of coffee. Remember the famous line, "Coffee is for closers," from the legendary sales movie *Glengarry Glen Ross*?

That was a great movie line, but the reality is coffee, actually caffeine, is an abused stimulant. You know caffeine will provide an initial jolt of energy, but it always leads to the inevitable crash shortly after.

If you want to keep your energy levels consistent at the agency, limit the amount of caffeine you pump into your body each day. If you enjoy the taste of coffee, consider switching to decaf in the afternoon or do some research into mushroom coffee, which gives you some of the flavor and same energy benefits without the caffeine.

Breath in Breath Out

Breathing is important. A human can live three days without water but only three minutes without air. Hands down, the one daily discipline that I share with my mastermind group which has made the biggest difference in my life is meditation. Like many people, I had a fear and confusion around the practice. I thought meditation was a practice of sitting in silence trying not to think about anything. As soon as a thought popped into my head, I lost.

It's the opposite. Meditation teaches you to stay centered, focused, and present in each moment. When thoughts pop in your head, and they will, meditation teaches us to acknowledge the thought and then file it away so we can remain focused on the main priority, which, during the meditation practice, is your breathing. I use a free app on my iPhone which provides a different guided meditation each day in 10 minutes or less.

Where this practice helps us within the insurance agency is our ability to optimize every opportunity that presents itself each day. When you slow down, stay present, and live in each moment, you recognize, optimize and then capitalize on opportunities you would have otherwise missed. We talk a lot at my agency about impermanence. The present is all that matters and living in the moment allows you to see all opportunities, which is true opportunity optimization.

Yesterday's gone and tomorrow is not guaranteed, so the now is all we ever get in life. Too many insurance producers dwell on the past, a customer who said no, or a prospect who didn't buy, or a word track that fell flat. Too many producers fear the future. How will they hit their goals? What if somebody doesn't show up? What if a customer says no again? Between living in the past and the stressing about the future, they miss all the opportunities that are right in front of them.

Focus on your breathing, stay present in each moment, and understand that everything you can control is right in front of you and it's happening right now.

Chapter 4:
Your Mission, Purpose, and the Why

Every company has a mission statement. Your agency has a mission statement, or at least I hope it does. The question is, do you know it? If not that's a problem, if you're stepping foot into an agency where you are earning a living and your role is to produce at a high level and grow that agency and make it profitable, but you have no clue what the mission of the agency is, then how on God's green earth are you going to move towards it?

By definition, a mission is a critical task that must be carried out. If you are on a mission, you are a person possessed to accomplish whatever the mission requires of you. How can you be on a mission if you have no clue what that mission is?

What is your mission statement? If you don't have one, you're about to. If you do have one, but it doesn't roll off your tongue as your name and address does, then you need to work on that today.

The biggest problem I see when it comes to mission statements is they're way too long. They often use words that aren't part of our everyday vocabulary, and many times, they sound great when you read them, but then they don't move people to action. Here are the most important questions you can ask yourself.

- What makes your agency different?
- Why do your customers love you?
- When price is not a factor, why do prospects choose you over the competition?
- Why do you love working there?
- What makes you the best possible option for the customers you serve?
- Why do you get out of bed each morning and go to work?
- What do you want to accomplish with your work?
- What do you want your legacy at the agency to be?

I want you to put some time and thought into these questions and your corresponding answers. Initially, speedily write the first draft.

Whatever comes into your head, regurgitate it on the paper. Then, keep that list in front of you and add to it throughout the day. Chat with other people in the office to hear their answers, and ask customers why they choose to do business with you and what they like most about your agency. Then add that to the list.

All day long, I want you to dig deeper into these questions. I want you to seek the answers to these questions and write them down. This is our agency mission statement:

> *Our mission is to be different. Each day, we will do the little things that others don't, and others won't. This will allow us to help more people in more ways forever.*

Here's my take on the insurance industry: It's overly commoditized. We sell a promise and humans are not built to get overly excited about a promise. We rely on our senses to guide us. We like shiny things. We like things that smell good. We like things that make us feel good, make us feel comfortable, make us look good, make us feel special. When we go to a car dealership, the number one goal is to get you behind the wheel. When you go to a high-end clothing store, the number one goal is to get you to try things on. When you go to a grocery store, they pump bakery smells throughout the store because people buy more when they feel at home, and they're hungry. Our products and services do not offer that sensory and emotional connection, so it's imperative that we create it.

Take a look at the answers to those questions as they pertain to the agency. What trends and themes do you see? Where are you now, and where do you want to be? Take the next 60 seconds, close your eyes, and visualize the future. Put yourself in the future. One year from now, you had the best year ever, and now you're looking back on it. You hit every goal you set. You qualified for every program and promotion you wanted. Your commissions and bonuses were your highest of all time.

Visualize how you feel, how you look. See the smile on your face, the sparkle in your eye, the peaceful easy feeling in your belly. Now look back on the best year ever and envision what it looked like. What did you do differently to make it the best? What did every single customer interaction look like? What did it sound like? Why were so many people excited to do business with you?

When you open your eyes, jot down everything you saw happening while you were looking back at your best year ever. Based on your answers from where you are now and your answers to how you envisioned your best year ever, now you can write a pretty kick-butt mission statement for your agency.

Mine is three short sentences. Sentence one is, "Our mission is to be different." When a customer walks into my office, I want them to think, "Damn, I'm so glad I do business here." The experience we provide should be different than any other agency around. It's not our goal to be *better* at what the competition does, but rather to be the *only* agency doing the things we do.

Sentence two is, "Each day, we will do the little things others don't, and others won't."

- Does the outside of the office look warm and inviting?
- When they walk in, does it smell like home?
- Are they greeted in a caring, sincere, professional manner?
- Are they thanked for coming in?
- Are they offered a drink or snack?
- Are they engaged in meaningful conversation?

Sentence three is, "This way, we can help more people in more ways forever." Part of my mission is to be so outrageously incredible at what we do that we earn the referrals of everybody's friends, families, and coworkers. This is how we're going to help more people and grow exponentially. In more ways, we are a multi-line agency. This means we have an abundance of opportunities beyond what most people even know about, and it's our job to educate them.

I absolutely love the word "forever," because it's the only amount of time we get. Our mission is not to help people for three to five years; it's forever.

Your mission statement is crucial. I want you to finalize it, write it down, print it out, post it where it's visible in the office, role play it, say it together as a team over and over again until it rolls off the tongue. Don't be afraid to share it with your customers. We tell our customers and prospects as often as we can, "Our mission is to be different. Each day, we do the little things that others don't and others won't. We want to help more people in more ways forever." What's your mission?

The Law of Attraction

My life changed forever in 2006 when I was introduced to the law of attraction. This is the concept that the universe sends us exactly what we ask it for. The thoughts in our heads will become the things in our lives, and you will ultimately possess whatever it is that you obsess about the most. With that in mind, you have to be extremely cautious of which thoughts you allow to reside in your head.

Create a vision board, and make it extremely specific. Keep your goals and visions for the life you desire in front of you and play out those visions in great detail every single day.

Again, back to the professional athlete, they work with sports psychologists at great length on visualization. They see themselves winning that trophy or making that shot.

Your Purpose, Passion & WHY

To discover your true WHY, I encourage you to dig deeper. When people are asked for their why or passion or purpose, most give a surface answer such as, "I want to make money, be a great parent, own a nice home, be a community leader, et cetera." Those are surface answers. Try to dig at least six levels deep to uncover your true why. You do this by asking the question, "Why," six times. I'm going to share with you how this exercise went when I went through it.

I want to help others improve themselves.

- *Level one.* Why? So they can be happier and help others whom I can't.
- *Level two.* Why does that matter to you? I believe helping, kindness and positivity has a ripple effect and spreads exponentially.
- *Level three.* Why does that matter? Through my efforts today, somebody will pay it forward tomorrow, and when this continues to happen repeatedly, eventually, somebody down the line who was helped will pay it forward back to me. It's karma.

- *Level four.* Why is karma important? It creates a cycle of when you always do the right thing then good things happen. With that in mind, if I'm always doing the right thing, then I'm the best possible version of myself.
- *Level five.* Why do you want to be the best version of yourself? I want to live a life of significance knowing my work here positively impacted tens of thousands of people directly or indirectly.
- *Level six.* Why is living a life of significance important to you? You only get a limited number of days to live, but you have an eternity to be remembered.

Boom, there's my answer: *My why is legacy*.

My purpose and passion is to help others so I can live my best possible life, give the most of myself knowing good things will always come back to me while I'm here on earth. In doing so, I leave an eternal impact long after I'm gone. That is what drives me to jump out of bed each morning, tackle each opportunity I have, and win every day that I'm so blessed to receive.

What is your why? What will you discover when you peel back six layers deep?

Chapter 5:
Creating a Winning Office Culture

We start here with optimizing every opportunity. If I were forced to name one thing my team does consistently which gives them a high level of results, it would be optimizing opportunities. Through the years, I've given this mindset a few different names. Initially, "The Plus-One Approach," which is to say, do what the customer is asking for, and then you add at least one more thought or question for them. Then I went to "thinking beyond the transaction," which was to remind us that customers call or come into the agency with a transaction in mind: to make a payment, update information on file, change a vehicle, or whatever else it might be. It's the job of my team to think beyond that transaction for an opportunity that may exist in addition to that transaction.

That leads us to today, where my latest name for this is "Opportunity Optimization." At the end of the day, it doesn't matter what you call it, but like everything else in this book and even more so with this Opportunity Optimization mindset, you have to take action.

A reporter once asked Hall of Fame baseball player Joe DiMaggio why he played so hard every day. His answer was, "Because there may be somebody in the stands that day who has never seen me play before or may never see me play again."

Think about how powerful that mindset is. DiMaggio was an opportunity optimizer on the baseball field every single day because he owed it to the fans in the stands to see the very best version of himself. Don't your policyholders deserve the 100% very best efforts that you can give each day, too?

Keep in mind that we are a modern-day society doing business differently than ever before. The value placed on personal relationships is lower than ever. People are communicating via electronics more than ever. Frankly, the insurance companies themselves are pushing people in that direction too. Customers want to do things themselves online or through an app.

They want text or emails with quick answers instead of in-depth conversations. If their cell phone rings and it's a number and not a name, they don't answer it. Think about it. Do you? I don't, either.

Think about how difficult it is in our industry to get in front of our very best customers. Who do we want to insure the most? Typically, it's people who are 25 to 60 years old, have jobs, own homes, have children, good credit, pay their bills every month, never have claims, and change vehicles once every three to five years. Those perfect demographics describe people who NEVER call or stop into our agencies.

We are doing business during a time when customers want to serve themselves online. They don't see the value in the face-to-face conversations as they did in the past. Those we most want to talk to the most rarely call or stop by. Then, when this perfect customer does call or stop in for something transactional to make a payment for example or update a credit card on file, why do we complete the transaction and say goodbye?

Once the transaction ends, you may not see or hear from that person for three more years. Worse yet, you know who wants to insure that person outside your agency? The answer is every other insurance producer in your state.

It's crucial that you provide a level of value that sets you apart with every customer interaction you have. If they walk in and out or call in and end that call and the only thing you talked about was a service transaction, you lose!

You must start thinking like an opportunity optimizer. It makes no difference how the opportunity begins. It can be a call about a rate increase, a claim, a general question, a complaint about billing. There are no bad opportunities. The only bad opportunities are the ones you fail to optimize by not taking action.

My producers absolutely love answering the phones and greeting people who walk through the door. Why? They don't see service as a burden but rather as an opportunity to talk to somebody about something. Why in the world would you want to waste your time making 50 outbound calls and talking to voicemails all day rather than optimizing the opportunities provided when the phone rings and when people are walking in?

There is a 100% chance that the person calling or walking in wants to talk to you.

Service is like breathing or walking. You can do it without thinking about it. Where producers take their production to the next level is when they go beyond the transaction with a transition statement. It's crucial for you to create a *transition statement* that you are comfortable with and, more importantly, one that you will use with absolutely everybody you talk to all day long.

What is a transition statement? When you finish something transactional, you then transition by saying something like, "Okay, I took care of such and such, but oh by the way, when was the last time we sat down for a policy review?" Or, "Okay, I took care of such and such, but while I have you here, how come we protect the things you own but we don't protect you personally?" Or, "Okay, I took care of such and such, but while I have you on the phone, do you mind if I take a second to verify lien holders on your home and auto as well as beneficiaries on your life insurance?"

Each person you interact with today is an opportunity. Make sure you give them 100% of yourself. It may be the only opportunity you have with them for years to come or ever again. Write your transition statement down, keep it in front of you and then use it all day today.

Opportunity Optimizing

There's an insane amount of information you have right in front of you as a multi-line insurance producer, but oftentimes, you don't do anything with it. When a customer trades in their two door coupe for a minivan, should that raise a red flag? Is there a possible life event there, or do you think they feel cooler in a minivan? How about when a customer still has full coverage on a 25 year old vehicle? Is it time for a review, perhaps?

When a customer has different liability limits or deductibles on different vehicles or when they call, and they tell you they paid off a loan on a vehicle, do you think they have a few extra dollars available in their budget now? It's also crucial to verify lien holders. "Do you still have that loan with ABC Bank? You do? When was the last time you shopped to make sure you have the best financing option available?" The same goes for home insurance.

Always verify the mortgage information. You can use that to spark a conversation about plans for the home. How many years do they have left on the mortgage? How much do they still owe on the mortgage? How are they protecting that mortgage if their income is suspended or goes away forever? Ask them about their occupation.

Do they have a pension? If so, schedule a review so that you can see what you can offer regarding taking the maximum pension benefit available once they retire.

Going back to homes, have a go-to endorsement that you'd like to review with them or ask them to come in to give you all the updates they've made to their home since you wrote it to make certain they will have full replacement cost. These are opportunities that you'll have to dig deeper for, but how about the slam dunks that are right in front of your face? I once had a team member who was helping a new mother with a car change. I knew she was a new mother because she was holding a one-month-old baby. When the new mother left, I asked my team member when was her appointment to review life insurance options, to which she replied, "I didn't ask." Unfortunately, this opportunity wasn't the right fit for that team member.

I challenge you to write down all the different opportunities you have right in front of you when a customer calls or walks in. The problem is, as humans, we oftentimes have tunnel vision. We get so caught up in the transaction that we miss the opportunity that's right in front of us.

Competition

In a field of black, white and brown cows, the easiest way to stand out from the rest is to be a purple cow. This is a famous advertising and marketing approach introduced by Seth Godin's book, *Purple Cow: Transform Your Business by Being Remarkable.* In the book, he notes that creative advertising is less effective today because there's so much clutter. Because of this, consumers tend to avoid or ignore advertising altogether.

In order to make an impact within your market, it's crucial that your agency becomes a purple cow and stands out from the rest who are still using the same old techniques.

Your agency must be the one thing required to stand out from the rest and dominate in your market space. It must be different. It's no secret that we operate in a highly competitive, highly regulated, and highly commoditized space. Customers don't understand insurance; most don't like insurance, and most have no clue why one company or different coverages are better than others. The only thing you have which makes you different and separates you from your competition is YOU

Your competitors don't have you. They don't have your team. They don't have your winning office culture. You are different. You are better because you commit to continuous improvement through books such as this.

Now you have to go out and tell people that you are different and start proving your value. The large insurance companies take care of national advertising. What does that leave for you? It leaves you what I call grassroots marketing.

Today, I want you to think outside the box and start creating a list of ways you can get your name/face in front of potential customers and referral sources in a different fashion. Some of the things we've done at my agency include holding client appreciation events such as brunches, cookouts, carnivals, ballgames. No strings attached. It's a way to say thank you and enjoy a fun afternoon with the people who support your business. Referrals always spike through the roof the week following these events.

I also believe in what I call next-generation marketing, meaning I get heavily involved in the schools. Whether it's teen driving programs, career days, or volunteering at school events, each year, I meet with principals, superintendents and PTO groups letting them know that anything they need help with, I'm their guy.

It's the same for local police and fire departments. When they hold their safety and prevention programs, we are there. I've also discovered that feeding people is a great way to earn their business. When teachers have conference days, I'll cater lunch.

When car dealers, realtors, or mortgage brokers hold their morning meetings, we stop by with coffee, donuts, pens, pads, calendars, business cards, or other agency items.

Speaking of coffee, we've done cross-promotions with other small businesses, one of them being a local coffee shop, that we set up a date and time with, such as Monday morning 8:00 to 9:00 AM, where people can stop by and get a free coffee, compliments of our agency. During the days leading up, we cross-promote each other.

When the customer shows up, we're saying hi and allowing them to thank us for buying their coffee.

For another cross-promotion, we send every single customer in our book a hand-signed birthday card. We partner with a local business to provide them with a free birthday gift. In the past, we've done a free pizza, free appetizer, or free dessert at a local restaurant. It costs us nothing because we're mailing the birthday cards anyway. The restaurant owners love it because it allows them to mail a coupon to people for free and it draws them to their establishment to celebrate their birthday dinner.

That is the one I get the most feedback from. Every place I go, I'm thanked for the birthday card. People call the office to thank me. They send thank you cards. They post on social media thanking me. Oftentimes, my wife and I will dine at the same restaurant, so we conveniently run into people who can thank us in person.

Other grassroots marketing involves making sure every single sub shop, pizzeria, gas station, and hair salon have our pens. Any place I use a credit card within a 10-mile radius of my office, I want to sign that receipt with one of my pens. We also post flyers on every community board. Again, the point is to be different, to stand out like purple cows.

I love when people tell me they're sick of seeing my name and face everywhere they go. That is how I know my marketing is working. The entire goal around advertising and marketing is top-of-mind awareness. You want to be the first agency people think of when they decide to shop their insurance. You must make your agency different to stand out in a highly competitive, highly commoditized industry.

Step one is to make your marketing so different that they call or stop in, but then step two is to make your customer's experience so different that they realize your value and not only want to do business with you, but they also want to refer friends and family to you. You need to shop your competition, it will force you to stop and ask yourself, "Am I that different from them?"

Simply thinking that you are doesn't mean that you are. When it comes to your customer experience, what matters most is consistently executing on the little things with every single customer interaction. While you can certainly do big-splash events to set your agency apart from the competition, understand you don't have to do big things in order to make a big impact.

Here's how we separate ourselves. For starters, we make sure the exterior of our building and grounds are clean and aesthetically pleasing.

When people come into the entrance way, we have a sign saying, "Welcome to our agency," and then it continues with our mission statement. We make sure the temperature is comfortable, the lighting is bright, and there are warm, comfortable aromas in the air.

If we know the customer's name, we stand up and greet them by name. If we don't, we still stand up, and greet them with a smile and ask, "What brings you in today?" Don't be the person who sits at the desk and barks out, "How can I help you?" Let your competition do that.

If they say they're looking for a quote, we respond with excitement. "Fantastic. Who referred you to our agency?" We'll get into referrals later, but this question allows you to set the expectation and explain that you are a referral-based agency.

No different than a guest in your home, you stood up, smiled, greeted them warmly. Now what? Offer to take their coat. Offer them a beverage or a snack. Our office is basically a convenience store. We have water, soda, juice, chips, candy bars, gum, Tic Tacs, mints, cookies, popcorn. Whatever somebody wants, they get it.

We then start the process of either getting to know our guest, or if we already know them, we start the process of getting to know them better. That is the "opportunity optimization" process.

Another thing we do is to make sure that everyone leaves with a small gift. It may be a pen or a calendar or something seasonal like an ice scraper or a koozie. If they have children, we offer crayons and coloring books.

The final thing we do before they leave is express gratitude. We look them in the eye, and we say, "Thank you for stopping in today. We know you have many insurance options, and we're glad you chose us or we're glad you trust us with your business." We walk them to the door and open it for them. Again, nothing in this process is complicated. None of it includes things that you cannot do every single time, but the question is, do you do them?

A snapshot of your competition is as follows: a customer walks in, a preoccupied team member looks annoyed that the person is there and barks out, "Can I help you?" Customer says, "I need to make a payment." They bark back, "Name?" Customer gives the name, team member gives the amount due, they process it, and the customer leaves.

Here's a snapshot of your agency when you cut through the clutter. A customer approaches a clean building, walks into a well-lit, great-smelling office. They're greeted by name. Team member stands up, smiles, welcomes them. They are asked what brings them in to visit today; they're offered a snack or a beverage before they sit.

As the customer's making their payment, the team member takes an interest in them, asks questions, makes sure their account is in perfect order, and before they leave, they give them a small gift. Then they walk them to the door, and as the team member opens the door for them, they look them square in the eyes, and they say, "I want to say thank you. We know you have several options when it comes to insurance. We're so glad you chose us."

Stop Believing it's ALL about RATE

In order to find the level of success you desire as an insurance producer, you must stop talking about rate. Stop trying to budget other people's money for them. Stop deciding and thinking that the only thing the person in front of you cares about is the rate. Let the lazy order takers who work for the competition keep talking about rate.

They're human robots who offer no value. They read questions on the application and then spit out an answer at the end, and if the rate is lower, they might write a policy. Honestly, when you break down that process, where is the value? What is the need for that insurance producer?

Unless the person on the other end of the phone cannot read, then there's no purpose for that call because the customer could've done the same thing online by typing in the answers themselves. No. They made an effort to call the place they thought was going to be a professional insurance agency, and then they got a person who read them application questions and spit out a rate at the end. If you are going to keep making this industry about nothing more than rate, then you're going to keep losing more than you win, and you're going to hate your job (or at least you should).

Think of yourself as a consumer. Do you buy exclusively on rate? Are the clothes you're wearing today all from secondhand stores? How about the car you drove to the office today? Was it the cheapest possible option out there? Did the toilet paper in your bathroom cost 23 cents a roll? Why not? Clothes are clothes, cars are cars, and TP is TP, right? No, it's not right.

*Remember, price only matters
in the absence of value.*

In 2001, Kelly my now wife, and I had been dating for more than three years. We had moved into an apartment together in Virginia. I knew this was the person I wanted to spend the rest of my life with. I wanted to buy an engagement ring and propose, but I had one problem. I was broke.

I had no money. I had a job and some credit, but I knew paying for this ring was going to be an uphill battle for me.

The first place I went was to a bargain jewelry store that constantly ran advertisements about how their pricing was the lowest and nobody could beat what they could sell for. That certainly sounded like the place for me, so off I went. When I pulled up to the store, the outside of the facility was dirty, papers littered the lawn. There were five exterior windows, one of which was cracked.

I walked in and found the showroom to be dark and dirty. The glass cases were smudged with fingerprints. Out from the back came a guy whose name I can't remember, but he looked like a Bruno. Gold chains around his neck, collar unbuttoned, stain on his shirt, and he was wiping part of his lunch from his mouth when he looked at me and asked, "What can I get you, guy?"

I told him I was looking for an engagement ring. He said, "Great," and proceeded to tell me that they have the best prices in town, and they can beat any of the other competitors' prices, and I shouldn't get too caught up in the four Cs that the other places are going to talk about. He assured me that "my lady" would love the size and sparkle of what he could sell me at a fraction of the price as everyone else.

I picked out a ring that was $1,500, and I told him I'd have to think about it. I left that jewelry store and felt like I needed a shower. I asked one of my coworkers the next day if she could recommend a jewelry store. She said, "Oh my God, absolutely. I love my jewelry store. They're called Personal Touch Jewelers, and when you go there, you have to ask for John."

I went to Personal Touch Jewelers. This time when I pulled up, the grounds were meticulous. When I walked in, the lighting was perfect, and the smells were inviting. I was quickly greeted by a friendly lady who said she would get John for me, but while I waited, she asked if I would like a drink. John was well-dressed in a suit and tie. He started asking me all about Kelly and her style. He took the time to get to know me by asking sincere questions. Then he took time to educate me on the different types of gold bands and quality of diamonds.

Along the way, he kept checking my understanding to make sure we were still on the same page, and that he was leading me in the right direction. Finally, we narrowed it down to the perfect diamond engagement ring. It cost $2,700, which was $1,200 more than Bruno's ring.

I was referred to Personal Touch Jewelers by somebody I trusted. I felt comfortable in their showroom. John spent an hour taking the time to make sure we picked out the perfect ring, but I was broke, and when I started this process, I thought it would be all about price. A ring is a ring, right?

Nope. That day, I was schooled on the power of value. Price didn't matter because I saw the value in doing business with John. I took out my credit card and bought the ring we selected on the spot.

What else did we buy through the years? We bought Kelly's wedding ring, my wedding ring, and then years later, anniversary bands as well as diamond earrings and necklaces. Also, I was in my mid-20s, and all of my friends were starting to get married. I sent John a ton of referrals. It's the same with jewelry sales, as insurance producers, we aren't in the *selling* business. We are in the *re-selling* business.

You might grab a quick sale today on rate, but without proving your value and taking the time to develop long-lasting relationships, you'll never make it long-term in this business. Don't jump over dollars to pick up dimes. You need to think about the amazing long game that our business offers.

Chapter 6:
Mindsets and Mantras

The number one reason people quit is they bail on faith. I'm not talking about religious faith, but rather the faith that all their small daily disciplines and activities are going to pay off in the future. They quit because they don't have faith in the fact, if they stick with this, they will find success.

They start to tell themselves they can't do something, or it's not worth their time, and the little things don't matter because 50 days into something, they aren't number one in the world for production numbers. As you're about to learn in this chapter, Mindsets and Mantras, our thoughts control our lives. The things we tell ourselves are the things we believe to be true, and they dictate our actions.

Our daily actions will ultimately determine our level of success.

This is known as a self-fulfilling prophecy. Those who quit on things stop believing their efforts are going to work, so then they stop working and, ultimately, their plan fails because they failed and quit trying. The irony here is many will quit and then they'll jump into some other system or training *du jour* or whatever product is guaranteeing them instant results.

Do you know what happens when they try that plan? They quit that, too, because what's broken is they lack the grit required to finish what they started. Successful people are obsessed with finishing. Unsuccessful people are obsessed with starting (and then complaining when things didn't work). Here's how the pyramid of success is designed for insurance producers.

The bottom of the pyramid is the widest. This is the biggest section because this is where everybody starts. Every year, there are tons of people who jump into this industry ready to make money, travel the world, and golf a lot. The next level up on the pyramid are those who make it through the first three years in this industry.

Unfortunately, most will not make it to this level. Most will quit in their first three years once they realize this business is hard. The people in this next group are now competing with fewer people at their level. They also have three years of experience and three years of practice and skills to make them more effective.

The third section of the pyramid is half the size of section two and only a quarter of the size of section one. These people are those who have been attacking this industry for six years, and guess what? Half of the people from section two don't make it here. Now there's even less competition of people with your skill set and experience.

The point of this is the longer you stick with something, not only do you get better, but the competition at your level gets smaller and smaller because, as the years go on, 90% of them quit. Fifty years ago, people got a job and stuck with it throughout their career.

Today, I get a resume from a 28-year-old, and they've already had five different jobs. What does that tell me? It tells me that person doesn't have the grit and faith required to grind it out; to learn the skills required to finish and succeed. The person with that resume is a starter. I want the 10% who can finish. If you are going to succeed at a high level as an insurance producer, you have to have stamina.

You have to take on the pain of more rejection. You have to have the patience required to master the mundane and do all of the little things. You have to develop more skills and have more work pride, and help more people in more ways every single day. To find success, you have to be the person who absolutely refuses to quit.

Do you know why people quit? Success requires work, and they don't want to put in the work required to change their habits. The 90% who quit do so because they say they want long-term success, but then they can't even put in the work required to get through reading this book. Do you want the million-dollar secret behind every single person who has ever succeeded at anything? It's only two words: Don't quit. Be the person who ignores instant gratification. Be the person who understands that there's no such thing as immediate results.

Be the person who fights through the pain of personal development, leave your comfort zone, do the things that you don't want to do, but you know you must every single day. Be the person who keeps climbing that pyramid after everyone beneath you has quit. Once you reach the top of the pyramid, you're now in the top 10%; it will all be worth the effort and sacrifice to get you there. Nobody told you this gig was going to be easy, but I'm here to tell you today that the climb will be worth it. Start to embrace the work and never quit.

What Are Your Sales Intentions?

Do the right thing for the right person at the right moment. That's it. When you do the right thing for the right person at the right moment, guess what? You can never be wrong.

Stop over-complicating the sales process. Your number one priority is to uncover and serve the needs of the person who's right in front of you in an ethical way.

Your prospects and customers have needs, concerns, or problems. Your job is to fully understand those needs, concerns, or problems and then solve them by offering a solution through a product, service, or advice. That's it. Don't over-complicate this industry. Let the 90% who get frustrated and ultimately fail with this gig keep making it complicated. You need to know what every other successful salesperson already understands and has mastered.

Our business is people helping people. Does somebody have a problem? We offer a solution. That's it. Too many salespeople get caught up in commission plans, tracking the numbers of calls they make, tracking the number of appointments they hold, trying to use slick talk tracks, or trying to manipulate people. Too many people try to cram a product down someone's throat when there is no actual need or reason for the person to have that product.

Do You Know Why People Hate Dealing With Salespeople?

Most of the people in our industry are doing exactly what I just described. Don't be that person. Instead, be the person who stands out as the purple cow. You don't have to have the latest and greatest word tracks or sales techniques or trick people into buying something you need to sell for a production goal, but they don't need in their life. I'm telling you right now, that is a recipe for disaster. If you are doing this business that way, you need to stop immediately.

I can honestly say in my 20 plus years of sales experience, I've sold real estate, mortgages, insurance, and financial services. I've been recognized in every one of those industries at the highest levels for production. While I always had a sales process, I've never once pushed anyone into buying anything. I've never had to use a hard close. I've never sold something to somebody which wasn't in their best interest.

Do you know what else I've never stressed about? I've never stressed about making my numbers or hitting my quotas, or achieving my goals in sales. Do you know why? When you do the right thing for the right person at the right moment, you can never be wrong. Consistently work that way and the numbers will always take care of themselves.

Catchphrases

If I spent one day in your office, what is the number one phrase I would hear over and over again? What's your battle cry when things get tough? What is your go-to phrase when there seem to be no answers or solutions to a problem?

In my opinion, every successful agency needs one or two. These phrases bond you as a team. They guide you as a producer. These phrases can be posted on your walls, shared in emails, and proclaimed to one another each day. We've had a few throughout the years at my agency, but one of the most recent, which I talked about earlier, is, "So what? Now what?"

On the surface, when you first hear it, it doesn't sound like much. To some, it might even sound like a cold phrase, but guess what? We are in a business for big boys and girls. We're in a business which isn't for the weak. We see people fail and quit in this industry every single day, and we live on a planet that keeps moving forward with or without us.

When something happens that you don't like and you aren't happy about, or you don't think is fair, so what? Now what? You can get over it and move on, or you can let time pass you by as you sit, pout and hold a pity party for yourself. Every single day at our agency, things change, or things happen that we wish didn't. That prospect stood you up for an appointment, this customer won't call you back, and you ran five quotes and couldn't sell any of them. So what? Now what?

A customer yelled at you over a billing issue. Another customer isn't happy with a claims experience. One of your biggest households got dropped. So what? Now what? The company took away or changed one of your favorite products. You didn't sleep well last night. You got stuck in traffic and spilled coffee on your shirt this morning. So what? Now what? Those four words are our go-to all day long.

If you're going to succeed at your agency, *it's crucial that you have a short-term memory*. Bad things and undesirable results will happen all day long. Those who can get over it and move onto something better the fastest, are those who will win every day. So what? Now what?

Here are a few others we've used in the past that are along the same lines.

- Tough times don't last, tough people do.
- Get it and forget it.
- And? (This one gets used when someone's complaining about something. It's more of an, "And...?")
- Next. (Something didn't go the way you planned? Next.)
- Chase the roar. (Scared of something in your day? Don't run away from it, run towards it. Chase the roar.)

Now it's your turn. Make this a fun office exercise. Think of all the different catchphrases and quick motivators you've used at your agency through the years and jot them down. Pick one or two of your favorites and use them all day long with one another.

Think Bigger and Break More Barriers

I love training people on proper mindsets and mental toughness. The biggest accomplishments I've seen with people I've trained and mentored throughout my career occur once they master their daily disciplines, learn to control their thoughts and maintain a positive/productive mindset.

Once you achieve THAT, then everything else starts to get easier. Training systems, processes, and word tracks are where everybody thinks it's at, but guess what? Our world is changing.

Our industry is changing. Our agencies are changing. Customers are changing. Everything is changing around us all the time, so the systems, processes, and word tracks you learn today will be obsolete tomorrow! Then, producers start chasing the latest and greatest trainings and seminars all over again.

What doesn't change is your mindset, attitude, grit, faith, and desire to win every single day!

When you master your mindset, stay true to your daily disciplines, and follow a consistent process, you will never fail.

We talked about not quitting; aligning your intent with what's best for the prospect or customer, office mantras and catch phrases to keep you on track and heading in a positive direction and stopping your negative self-talk. Now I want to share with you the power of thinking bigger and what happens once you break a barrier.

The day I opened my agency in 2009, I hung a picture of Roger Banister up, and underneath it, I wrote the words, "Nothing is possible until you believe that it is."

In my opinion, the story of Roger Banister and the four-minute mile is the greatest tale of conquering the odds when it comes to the power of limitations within the human brain.

In the early 1950s, Roger Bannister started training his body, and more importantly, his mind to run one mile in under four minutes. Up to that point in history, no human had ever been able to crack that time for that distance. In fact, many doctors believed that it was not safe for a human to push himself at that pace for that distance.

Doctors advised Bannister not to even attempt this because it could lead to his death. They believed his heart would explode at that pace for that distance.

Bannister did what all successful people do, he ignored the naysayers. On May 6, 1954, Bannister finished one mile in 3:59.4.

Not only did he not die (in fact, we didn't lose Roger until early in 2018 at the age of 88), but what happened NEXT is the true point to this story.

After Banister posted 3:59.4, it only took six weeks for somebody else to break his record, and then dozens of others ran sub-four-minute miles within the months after Roger broke that barrier.

The point is the human body could always do it. The problem was the human brain never believed it. Today, there are over 1,400 people who have accomplished this feat, including five boys in high school. The current record is 3:43.

I hung a picture of Roger Bannister in my office because I believed that if I thought bigger, I'd be able to break any challenge in my market.

My agency is in an extremely rural area in Central New York State. Our population is low, and our median household income is at poverty level.

When I opened, those around me said writing 40 new auto policies each month would be a great stretch goal, that hitting 30 would be more realistic. Me (and my picture of Bannister) thought that was great, but proceeded to set my monthly goal at 100.

People said I was out of my mind until four months later when we wrote 100. Then, we knew it was possible, so, for the remainder of that year, we wrote over 100 NEW auto policies every single month.

Almost 10 years later, we continue to be a leader in our territory with auto, fire, life, health, and bank production. I attribute much of this success to mindset and thinking bigger.

Most agencies in our market make it their goal to write 100 total policies each month. My team makes it their personal goal to write 100 policies each. Again, we know this is possible because my team members have done it. They've proved it to themselves, and now it's the standard.

Look at your current personal goals and the agency goals. Write them down and then double them. What you will see is a huge number, and you are immediately going to have a mental barrier telling you that you can't achieve anything even close. I'm here to remind you today that you can. I'm here to tell you that nothing is possible until you believe that it is. When you shoot for the moon and miss, you hit the stars.

If you want to produce at an insanely high level, you must start setting insanely high goals. Once you do and you stick with it and work towards the number in front of you, I promise that next year at this time, you'll not only be hitting that new goal, but you'll also be kicking yourself that you didn't set your goals higher years ago.

Avoiding Negative Self-Talk

I don't care if a person has a college degree, if they have 20 years' experience, if they have been through a dozen trainings and seminars, if they have memorized all the fancy word tracks, systems, and processes available today. If they have a negative mindset and a piss-poor attitude, I have no use for that person in my personal life or on my agency team.

Too many people work this business backward. They tell themselves that once they learn all the ins and outs of the industry and they figure out what the most successful producers are doing and saying, then they will be happier and produce at a higher level and realize long-lasting success.

They are wrong. Stop poo-pooing the fact that your <u>mindset is everything </u>when it comes to health, happiness, and overall productivity. Those who are most successful with everything are those who *think better* than everybody else.

Give me a person with no education, no industry experience, and no professional training but has a positive mindset, a desire to continuously improve, a willingness to take immediate action on the little things and do so consistently.

Give me a person who has grit and faith and an unquenchable thirst to win at everything they do, and I will take that person in my life and on my team all day long.

I want each of you to be that person, but you cannot be that person if you don't believe you are that person first.

If I had to name one thing that prevents people from attaining higher levels of success, it would be negative self-talk.

How many times have you been in the middle of something and thought to yourself, "I can't do this," or, "I'm not good enough to do that," or, "I'm not smart enough to do this," or, "I don't have what it takes to be that." Worse yet, forget being in the middle of doing something with those thoughts. How many times have you never even started something because of your negative self-talk?

I tell people all the time in my trainings that when I see the words, "I can't (I-C-A-N-T)," I see somebody who is kicking their A out and leaving themselves with I-C-N-T, which is an acronym for, "I Choose Not To!"

It's not that you can't do anything. If you're honest, it's that you choose not even to try.

You <u>can</u> optimize every single opportunity. You <u>can</u> ask for a review appointment. You <u>can</u> ask people to protect their life and their income.

You <u>can</u> ask people for the names of their friends and family. You <u>can</u> create a higher-level customer experience. You <u>can</u> express your gratitude. You <u>can</u> forgive and forget. You <u>can</u> stick to your daily disciplines. You <u>can</u> create an action plan to win every day, and you <u>can</u> follow the sales process you'll learn at the end of this book 100% of the time.

However, when you don't, it's not that you can't. You are simply choosing not to.

As a licensed insurance producer, you know 95% more than the person sitting in front of you or on the other end of that phone, but too many times, you allow negative self-talk to hold you back from doing everything you know you need to do and say.

You are where you are today because somebody believed in you. Now, you need to believe in yourself as much. You have more to offer than you believe you do or perhaps even realize you do. Other people need to hear your voice and your message.

There are some producers in this industry who couldn't sell $100 bills for 50 bucks because their brains prevent them from succeeding.

They sabotage themselves with fear and negative self-talk, and they justify their roles at the agency with "busy work." Don't be that person. When you choose to focus on and improve your strengths, you can overcome any of your perceived weaknesses.

Chapter 7:
Plan, Prep, Keep Score, and Win Every Moment

Why We Fail

If we are going to change our results, we must first change our mindsets and habits. It's as simple as that. I've already given you the big secret as to why people fail in this industry. They keep working this business the same exact way the people who failed before them did! Then, they quit shortly after these broken techniques do not lead them to the success they desire.

The definition of insanity is doing the same thing over and over again and expecting different results. You have to change the way you approach your customer interactions from the very first time you speak to them as a prospect.

I talk to agents and team members every single day and regardless of rural, metro, new market agency, assignment agency, rich community, poor community, it makes no difference.

The same struggles every single one of them shares are as follows (and tell me if any of this sounds familiar):

1. Auto rate is not competitive.
2. Even if it's close, we can't close without savings.
3. People don't want or can't afford life and health.
4. Tough to get people into the office; they want to do things over the phone.
5. People aren't giving me referrals.
6. Customers won't answer their phones when we call for annual reviews.
7. When people come in for annual reviews, they aren't buying anything else.

Do any of those sound familiar?

The good news is you're not alone. The better news is what I'm about to share with you will fix all those problems. The best news is once you embrace what I'm about to tell you and take immediate action on it by practicing until you master it (and fighting through the initial trial runs when you will suck at it), your production numbers will go through the roof, and you'll love coming to work every single day.

You must erase your memory because, through no fault of your own, you have learned so many bad habits when it comes to providing long-term solutions for all your customers' needs. You have been working backward, but it's not you. It's the entire insurance industry.

Somewhere along the line, we forgot there is a natural order to sales. There is a specific process we must follow. Somewhere along the line, we forgot that customers today are smart. We now live during a time of tremendous information availability and in a consumer-savvy society.

It used to be people depended on salespeople to educate them and guide them.

Now, consumers do plenty of their own research before they start shopping. They've seen and heard it all from poor salespeople with cheesy one-liners and lousy canned word tracks. They view salespeople as slimy, unethical people who shouldn't be trusted. Honestly, in many cases, they are right.

Why, then, in the insurance industry, do we continue to do business like it's 1989? A customer calls for a quote. The salesperson reads them the questions, inputs the answers, and then clicks the button at the end. If the rate comes back the same or higher than what the customer has now, the salesperson thanks them for their time and pends for follow-up. Then, for the next five years, that prospect never answers your call again because, in their heads, your company is more expensive, so there's no need to talk.

How about this? The salesperson clicks the button, and yeah, they are $40/month less. YIPPEE!!! They tell the customer, "Based on the same "apples to apples" comparison to your current policy, we can save you almost $500/year!"

What happens next? They want to bind it over the phone, and you have no opportunity to show them any other ways you're able to protect their family properly. Maybe they do come in, and by the time they get to your office, they have already spent that $500 five times over. Now, you start your sales pitch to them with your fancy pictures and canned word tracks, and they shut down because they don't want to get sold anything else.

You know who else does this? The car industry. You pick out the car. You're happy with the price, and then, what comes next but a conversation with the F&I guy, with all his undercoating and warranties and protection products that you don't want to spend another $40/month on. You hate the F&I guy, but at the agency, you set yourself up as one when you give prospects the price and then try to explain other options they have once they get there.

Then, you complain you can't get referrals. You offer them a gift card for coffee or $10 on a Visa and desperately beg for names of the people closest to them, but honestly, do you deserve them? What did you do?

You entered data, clicked a button, gave them the exact same thing they already had for less money, made a halfhearted attempt to offer some other products after it was too late, you printed some paperwork, and then proposed to trade a $10 gift card for the names and phone numbers of the people they love most in this world.

Think about all of that and let it sink in.

Then, once they ARE a customer, you chase them forever for a review. Do you know why they don't want to come in for a review?

It's simple:

1. They don't want to be sold anything by somebody they don't know or trust.
2. (And this one may sting) They don't know and trust you.

Finally, they leave your agency as soon as somebody else beats your rate with the same coverage.

Words Matter

As an insurance producer, you talk to people ALL day long. However, do you pay attention to the words you are using? If an artist needs paint & canvas, a chef needs food, and a mechanic needs tools, you need words to be successful at your craft. You need to choose them wisely.

I want to review some power words that you can start incorporating into your everyday vernacular.

Amazing: Everybody wants to be amazed. It tugs on people's emotions and makes them move to take action.

If I told you a dinner or show was <u>amazing</u>, would you be more interested than if it were good or even great?

"Mr. Customer, I'd like to meet with you to review some <u>amazing</u> opportunities we have for you at the agency."

Avoid: The fear of missing out is real. People will take action to <u>avoid</u> missing something quicker than they will to gain something. Use the word "avoid."

"Mr. Customer, I'd like to meet with you this week because it's my job to help you <u>avoid</u> the potential losses that we see so often at claims time."

Because: The word "because" explains the why behind people's need to take action.

"Mr. Customer, I need to meet with you this week <u>because</u> we have seen an incredible number of losses within our community recently, and I want to help you <u>avoid</u> getting stuck in a bad situation."

(See what I did there? I threw in two words at no extra cost!)

First: Everybody wants to be first: <u>first</u> place, <u>first</u> prize, or the person who gets told <u>first</u>. It shows priority, makes them a VIP.

"Mr. Customer, I only have time in my schedule to meet with 20 customers this month, but before I start filling in dates and times, I wanted to call you <u>first</u>."

Solutions: The bottom line is people want solutions to their biggest problems, and they want answers to all their questions.

"Mr. Customer, based on what you are telling me is important to you, I've come up with a couple different <u>solutions</u> for you to consider."

Options: Nobody wants to be told they have to do something. Everybody wants <u>options</u>.

"Mr. Customer, based on everything you said was important to you, it looks like I have two, three, maybe even four <u>amazing options</u> for you to consider. The <u>first</u> thing we'll need to do is schedule a time to meet. How soon can you come in?"

(Three power words there!)

Imagine: We sell products that help people when they need it the most. However, it's not something people see, touch, feel, or smell, so they have to <u>imagine</u>.

"Mr. Customer, _imagine_ how _amazing_ it will feel to know that you are properly protected from all uncertainty."

Simple: There's a _simple_ explanation here. People like things that are easy. Remind them of how _simple_ working with you is.

"Mr. Customer, now that you have designed and customized your protection plan, putting it in place and starting it all today will be super _simple_."

We: These are two letters which are super powerful. _We_, not me. It lets the customer know that you two are in this thing together. When referring to your company, it's _we_, not they. When something needs to be done, it's _we_, not you.

"Mr. Customer, I'm glad _we_ met today, and I'm excited about servicing the _amazing_ plan _we_ built together for many years to come."

Optimal: You hear me talk about opportunity optimization all the time. The word "optimal" means "the best" or "most favorable." When you are speaking to a customer, don't you want your solutions to be the best?

"Mr. Customer, based on the concerns you shared with me, I was able to create an _optimal solution_ which allows you to _avoid_ potential future risks. Together, _we_ can get this _amazing_ plan started today _because_ it's extremely _simple_!"

Okay, so I threw seven power words in there. Overkill? You decide.

How about words we want to avoid?

Honestly implies you were lying before.

Buy: To buy is to be sold. Try "start" or "put in place."

Hope, think, should: You should never hope or think something will work. "You should be okay" is bad, too. This shows lack of confidence and uncertainty

Don't: Be careful how you position this: "You don't want to do that." Nobody wants to be told what they don't want to do in most cases.

Remember what's in it for them.

Obviously: This implies they should know something that they may not know. When you say "obviously," it makes people feel dumb and they may check out or like you less.

Cheap: You don't want to be cheap, do you? I hope not. What you want to do is offer more value.

Guarantee: Be super careful making promises you can't back up. Customers and prospects remember certain words 100% of the time. "Guarantee" is one of them which could come back to bite you.

Discount: I know. Our industry talks about discounts all the time, but this de-values you and your products and services. Instead of offering discounts, offer maximum value or maximize their savings.

Competitor: Get yourself into a mental state where you are your only competition. Don't bring up competitors because honestly, if you're doing your job right, they don't matter.

Any industry jargon, slang, or acronyms: We use them all the time when we communicate with one another. However, these words or acronyms mean nothing to your customers and prospects. Never use them.

List: Can there be anything less personal than "I'm calling because you were on my LIST"? Don't ever mention a list or tell people they are on one.

Finally, our industry products sound scary as hell to people.

Liability: Change that to "asset protection."

Drop: Change that to "non-renew."

Rate increase: Change that to "adverse action."

Life insurance: Change that to legacy money.

Disability insurance: Change to "income replacement."

Death: Change that to "the unthinkable."

Disabled: Change to "unable to work for a period of time."

Choose a few power words you will commit to using immediately. I know these will be uncomfortable in the beginning, but all change comes with some initial discomfort. Write some word tracks that include these words when it comes to scheduling appointments or within your sales process.

Next, take inventory of the negative words you currently use each day. Identify these, write them down and then work on eliminating them from your vocabulary. Words matter. You talk all day long. Your success will be determined by the things you say and also by the things you don't.

Radio Station WIIFM

I am broadcasting LIVE today from Radio Station WIIFM, the "What's in It For Me" station on your customer's dial.

That's all your customers care about and that's all you should care about, too. Too many insurance producers try to sell with their own best interest in mind and not the best interest of the person in front of them. That is a formula for failure.

Your goals, your quotas, your opinions on what you think is best for a customer do not matter in the sales process. The more you push your agenda on somebody, the less interested people are in doing business with you.

I learned this early in my sales career when I was at the furniture store after college. I quickly realized that my taste is not the same as everybody else's and that was okay.

In the insurance world, it is crucial you do a complete needs analysis to truly understand what is best for your prospects and customers. For example, say you complete the sales process and the customer chooses a life insurance product, but you need one more health product to maximize your comp plan for the month, under no circumstances should you ever steer them towards the product you need versus what they desire. This is unethical and it will come back to bite you somewhere down the road.

Again, when you do the right thing for the right person at the right moment, you can never be wrong.

WIIFM: What's in it for ME?

This is the question each customer or prospect is silently asking themselves. It is your job to provide them with the correct answer to that question.

I don't care if it's a new prospect, a current customer, a sales appointment, or somebody making a payment. Spend the time to ask the questions and uncover their why. Why are they doing business with you? Why did they call or stop in to see you?

Once you know what's in it for them, you can tailor your conversations and your sales process around that. Remember, you have to throw your ego and your agenda out the window when it comes to sales.

Once you align your sales intentions with their best interest, then you can optimize every opportunity and your production will soar.

What are You Tracking?

We track three things at my agency: the number of households you quoted, policies you wrote, and referrals you earned. I'm not telling you to stop using whatever product or system you use at your agency to track activity and production. What I am saying here is sometimes less is more.

I've built my entire career around keeping things simple (mainly because I was never smart enough to over-complicate things). With that being said, here is what we do in our agency:

- We talk to people.
- We express our gratitude.
- We prove we are better and different than our competition.
- We ask prospects and customers questions.
- We LISTEN to their answers.
- We uncover their needs.
- We offer a solution or solutions to best satisfy those needs.

That's it. It's super simple. We ask, listen, and optimize opportunities.

All we track are three things. How many households did we quote? How many policies did we write? How many referrals did we earn? Then, each morning, each team member declares their results to the team. They stand up and say, "I quoted this many households, I wrote this number of policies, and I earned this number of referrals yesterday."

Our office mantra is "Zero Zeros." If every single team member has at least one in each of those three categories every single day, we have won that day, and when we win each day, our monthly and annual goals take care of themselves.

Chapter 8:
The Sales Process

You're a producer in a MULTI-LINE agency, start acting like it. When you chose to be a producer with this opportunity, you knew you were going to have to sell more than just auto insurance if you were going to hit the numbers you needed to hit to create the income you wanted to earn. Am I right? Remember, you are an opportunity optimizer. The way I always optimized my opportunities in sales was by grabbing my compensation plan, dissecting it, and figuring out how to maximize it.

There is no possible way for me to know what each of your compensation plans looks like, but I'm willing to bet that you can make some money selling auto, but even more money selling auto, fire, life, health, and bank. Am I right?

Then why the hell are you talking to prospects every single day, and as soon as you cannot write their auto policy, you end the conversation and kill the relationship? You have to change your mindset. You have to approach each opportunity with the intent to share every single solution you can offer.

When I first opened my agency from scratch, I had zero customers, a wife, and two children. I knew that if I only spoke about home and auto to my new customers, I'd only be able to feed two out of three mouths in my house, and that wasn't going to be a long term winning formula. We are so fortunate, as multi-line producers, that people will give us an opportunity to talk to them because we offer car insurance, and every single car insurance provider spends billions of dollars each year to remind all of America that they should be shopping their car insurance. This provides you with the opportunity to *start* a conversation, but the car insurance should never be where your conversation ends.

There is an old cliché in our industry that we get into people's homes through the biggest door they have in the house: the garage door. When a prospect allows you through their garage door, they are looking for an auto quote because that's all your competition has ever done for them in the past. However, the true sales artists know that they hold the brush. It's their blank canvas, so they have control of the process.

Don't be re-active with your sales process, be pro-active. You have to guide the prospect down the path they need to go. If you allow them to tell you what to do, you lose control and you lose the sale.

Make the Invisible Visible

Storytelling is the most important tool in your bag. The art of storytelling is a game-changer for salespeople who understand and embrace this concept. What do we sell as insurance producers? Regardless of the product, ultimately, all we sell is a promise. A customer buys a policy, and if something bad happens, we promise to help them. That's it.

There are two huge problems when it comes to selling promises. They aren't sexy and they don't get people excited. Humans buy based on their emotional attachment to something. Emotions will always trump logic when it comes time for people to make a purchase. Also, consumers buy based off their senses. They like the way something feels or smells. They like the way something looks on them or in their home. They love the way something tastes.

Think about your last car-buying experience. The first thing that car salesman wants to do is what? They want to get you to test drive a vehicle. Why? It's super clean and people love that new car smell. They want you to feel how it accelerates so much faster than yours and how it handles when you turn the corner.

A car test drive puts you on sensory overload and ties you to that vehicle emotionally. Once you have to have it, the cost becomes secondary.

Therefore, the second problem we have trying to sell a promise to people is that it's not real. It's not something people can see, touch, feel, smell, or taste. They don't get excited about it, and most don't believe they'll ever need it. They have no emotional attachment to it.

I'm going to let you digest that concept because it's a big one. You must get into the heads and mindsets of your prospects if you are going to truly understand the why behind their decisions. Once you understand that promises aren't sexy, and on the surface, prospects have no emotional attachment, it's your job as a producer to bring these promises to life. The way ultra-successful salespeople have done this since the beginning of time is by harnessing the power of the story. It's a fact that top salespeople use an average of five stories within each sales presentation.

Let me share with you an amazing research project that was done on eBay not too long ago. A gentleman purchased 200 objects and spent under $2 for each of these objects. He then contacted a slew of writers and asked them if they would participate in his experiment to prove the power of the story in sales.

Each writer composed a well-thought-out, detail-specific story behind each of these items that cost less than $2. All 200 items were then listed on eBay with their stories.

The one that sold for the highest amount was a small plastic horse head. It cost 99 cents, but when the story was added, it sold for $62.95! I know what you're thinking. "Great, some idiot overpaid for one item. Nope. The other 199 items were all sold, and the total amount for those added up to shy of $8,000!

Two hundred items were purchased for $129. Those same 200 items, with great stories backing them, sold two weeks later for $8,000. The higher the emotional investment is, the less critical we become. People buy what they want, not what they need. For years, people have struggled as insurance producers because they are trying to sell features and explain to people why they need their promise. People fail in this industry because they don't grasp the concept of emotional attachment. The way we get people emotionally attached is by telling them a story.

Have you ever watched a movie? That's a rhetorical question. You didn't need to answer that one. Did you ever laugh, cry, feel sad, get angry, or all of those things in two hours or less? Sure, you've experienced all those emotions because you were fully engaged in the story. In fact, you were so engaged you were crying or angry over a character that doesn't exist.

You were so emotionally attached, after you left that movie, that you went out and purchased something that reminded you of that movie.

Perhaps it was a watch or an outfit or a car. Maybe you took a vacation or did something monetarily because of your emotional attachment to that story.

Do you know how I know this? Last year alone, companies spent over $11 billion on product placement inside movies. That's $11 Billion with a B, because they understand the power of emotional attachment. Think about a time you bought something you didn't need, but you made the purchase because you wanted it. Think about a story that pulled you in emotionally and made you make a purchase or send a donation. Then, start to think about some stories you can tell from your experience at the agency, a story of when you delivered on the promise you sold.

Components of a Great Story

I don't know about you, but no matter how many claims my customers are involved in, it is never, ever their fault. I can't tell you how many cars "just came out of nowhere" to hit my poor customers.

Therefore, rule #1 is to never, ever make the story about your customer and never ever make them at fault for anything. They can't wrap their brains around being at fault because they are perfect. Again, this is an area where insurance producers have been working backwards forever.

They start explaining coverage, and the first thing they do is talk about liability coverage. They say something along the lines of, "When you hit somebody and get sued, this is the money we have to protect you and your assets. God forbid if you kill or dismember the other driver or pedestrian. You could get sued for up to $1,000,000, and that's why you need a personal liability umbrella."

Whoa, whoa, whoa! Slow down! You lost that person, and whatever you say after that doesn't matter because they have checked out. "But Scott, that's all true. That is what liability coverage does." I know this, but there are a few major problems with the approach everybody seems to use.

First off, you made the accident their fault and they are never at fault. Don't believe me? Just ask them. They are "great drivers." Most will even proudly boast about their "perfect driving record." Then, you had them getting sued, so their heads are spinning already because they don't get into accidents to begin with, and now, they are getting sued. From there, you not only had them at fault, but they killed or dismembered another human. "Huh? Me? No way!"

Finally, you told them they need or should have a PLUP in case this disaster (which they don't think will ever happen), caused a seven-figure lawsuit. Remember, people buy what they want, not what they need. This person is sitting shaking their head thinking, "No way, not me." They now feel like you are trying to sell them something they do not need.

Never make your customer or prospect at fault while explaining coverages. Again, words matter. The number one thing humans fear the most and never want to do is die. Therefore, rule #2 is don't mention death or dying in any story. People don't want to die, and they don't want to kill others (well at least the ones you want in your book don't).

Rule #1: They are never at fault.

Rule #2: Don't kill anybody.

Rule #3 is to be as specific as possible.

Remember, a great story should pull somebody in, engage them, and allow them to picture the scene you are describing so they are there with the people you are talking about. When you craft your stories, be super specific. Use first names (not full names to protect the innocent). How old were they? What was their driving history? Where did they work? Exactly what road were they on? What were the exact circumstances that led up to the situation you're about to explain?

What were the exact results or consequences that came about as a result of that claim?

Then you have to do the number one thing required to improve: start practicing it immediately. You should be telling your stories so many times that you're repeating them in your sleep. Once you have them down, you can start working hard to perfect your delivery. What parts will you slow down through? Which parts will you stress for emphasis? Where will you pause for dramatic affect? Let's go! Start practicing.

Prescribe some Dopamine

When I was 26 years old, I was living in Northern Virginia. On this very day, I was across the Potomac on the 27th floor of an office building in Maryland. I was all alone, standing at the end of a long, bright hallway. My heart was racing. I was sweating. I was trying to calm myself through deep breaths because my hands were shaking. On the other side of that door were three men who were smarter, wealthier, and much more experienced than me. I knew I was going to have to shake each of their hands, and I didn't want to be shaking and sweaty when I did so.

I also knew that if I closed this deal, it would be the largest commission of my life and could change the direction of my young family for years to come. As I stood there trying to compose myself before grabbing onto that door handle and walking in, what I did not know at the time was that day would turn out to be the worst day of my life. But, I did not know that yet.

Finally, I wiped my palms on my suit pant legs. I started thinking positive thoughts. I convinced myself that I was ready for this moment that I had worked so hard to prepare for. I reached out to grab that door knob, and before I turned it, I heard a female voice call "Mr. Grates." It was the receptionist who had directed me to this long, bright hallway minutes earlier.

"Yes?" I replied with a cracked voice.

"There is something you need to know about these three men before you go in there and give them your pitch. I feel like I need to share something with you."

Now....are you curious as to what this lady needed to share with me at that very moment? I hope so. Would it be annoying if I never told you what she told me? I hope so. Because I'm not going to tell you. What I am going to tell you is this: What you experienced during that story was increased levels of dopamine sent by your brain via nerve cells.

During my story, was your focus increased? Was your attention increased? Did you create situations around this? Could you picture what that hallway looked like? What I looked like standing there sweating? What the 3 men on the other side of the door looked like? What the door handle I almost grabbed looked like?

Out of all that you will have read in this book, out of all you will learn during my trainings, I guarantee that this is one story that you'll remember more than most because you were engaged in the story, you could picture this all happening and you wanted to know what happened next.

A good story is designed to build suspense, keep people interested, and allow them to create a picture within their own heads.

A good story keeps us wanting to know what happens next. This is because a good story produces dopamine in the brains of the people listening. As an insurance producer who sells a promise, it's not sexy, it's not exciting, and it's not even real to many people. It is your job to prescribe what the doctor ordered, dopamine.

You must create that emotional attachment and increase the levels of dopamine in your prospect's brain through the power of story so they understand exactly what that promise is you're offering, how it works, why it works, and create a situation where the prospect wants to know more.

This way, by the end of the story, it won't be about them needing what you can offer. Instead, they will want what you have. That's when the magic happens because people buy what they want, not what they need. Just like you want to know what that lady told me that day, but I'm still not going to tell you!

The Sales Process, Step 1: The Open

The entire premise of "agency optimization" is to focus on doing all the little things consistently, over and over again, so that these seemingly insignificant activities compound into massive results. With that in mind, I kindly ask you to not dismiss anything in my TEN STEP sales process as insignificant. You might initially think you can skip over certain steps, but once you start using these steps, you'll discover how powerful they are.

The first step people try to skip is the very first one. Regardless of insurance sales or whatever else you are talking to somebody about, at the end of the day, we are all humans. We are all people, and people ultimately buy from people they like, people they trust, people they respect, and people who truly understand them.

Step 1 of the sales process is NOT to ask prospects for their name, address, and date of birth. That's like going out on a first date and before the server brings drinks to the table, you start talking about plans for marriage and children. It doesn't make sense, it's not logical, and frankly, it's awkward and weird.

The open is designed to let the prospect know that you care, that you are genuinely interested in helping them. You have to ask open-ended questions. Open-ended questions allow the prospect to speak freely. A closed question allows the prospect to give a one-word answer, which you want to avoid early in the process.

Some examples of open-ended questions are:

- What prompted you to call us?
- What's important for you to have at your next agency?
- Tell me a little bit about your family.

After you ask these questions, shut up and listen. Remember, you have two ears but only one mouth for a reason. You need to listen twice as much as you speak. The greatest persuasion tool you own are your ears, not your mouth. People love to talk about themselves, so let them. The number of questions you ask here is a judgement call. Sometimes you'll ask one and the prospect will speak forever. Sometimes you have to follow up with a few to get the conversation going.

Also, it is crucial you control your body language and tone. People respond so much more favorably to people who are happy, excited, smiling, and speak in a soft, sincere manner.

Have you ever seen somebody laughing uncontrollably? I'm talking on-the-floor belly laugh, with tears coming out of the eyes.

How do you react? Well, you start laughing, too! You don't even know what the other person is laughing about, but now you are, too. Why? We mirror what we see.

Body language, smiling, and voice inflection are super important. It doesn't matter if you're on the phone or in person. You sound better and people respond more favorably when you are smiling. Again, it's a judgement call how much time you spend on this step, but remember, those who fail in this industry do so because they are thinking backwards. They try to rush through the application, pray the rate is better, and then if it is, they write the business. Then, they try to build rapport at the end when they ask for referrals and, a year later, a review appointment. AHHHHH! Sorry, you're too late! You only get one chance to make a first impression. Within ten seconds, that prospect will have a good idea if they like you or not, so it's your job to give that prospect a reason to like you.

Express Gratitude

Now, the second part of Step 1: The Open is to show gratitude. This is a super quick one but outrageously important. People's time is precious. It's limited. It's the thing they value the most because they can't get more of it. Do you want to stand out? Do you want to stand alone and do something your competition isn't?

Do you want to get somebody to like, trust, and respect you immediately? All you have to do is express gratitude.

Part two is going to have you be sincerely appreciative even though you haven't asked your prospect for anything, and they haven't given you anything other than their time so far.

Address the prospect by name and say, "John, I know you have countless options when it comes to insurance. Regardless of who you choose to protect you, I want you to know I appreciate you giving my agency this opportunity today." Whoa! I'm sorry, what? You say that to another human (one who has a heartbeat) and tell me they aren't going to feel all warm and fuzzy on the inside.

Within the first couple minutes, you've built rapport by asking open-ended questions and listening to them share things about themselves, and then you followed that up by putting them at ease and expressing gratitude by saying, "Regardless of what you decide, I'm grateful you gave us an opportunity today."

I'm telling you right now, if you master step 1, it almost doesn't matter what comes next because this prospect is now rooting for you. They want to do business with you because nobody else is treating them like you did.

Step 2: Value Statement and Checking for Acceptance

Let's do a quick recap.

You spent a couple minutes building rapport. Then, you gave the prospect a sincere expression of gratitude.

Now, in Step 2, you are going to transition into your value statement.

"John, I'd like to share with you a little bit about how we do business here at our agency. We take great pride in being different than everybody else. It's the mission of our agency to go above and beyond, to do the little things other people don't, and other agencies won't. Our goal is to provide you with total protection, so when the unexpected does happen, you know you're properly covered."

That is my value statement. As soon as I finish that statement, I immediately check for acceptance. "*How does that sound?*" Here is the value statement again and my immediate checking for acceptance.

"John, I'd like to share with you a little bit about how we do business here at our agency. We take great pride in being different than everybody else. It's the mission of our agency to go above and beyond, to do the little things other people don't, and other agencies won't.

Our goal is to provide you with total protection, so when the unexpected does happen, you know that you're properly covered. How does that sound?"

What do you think the prospect's answer is to that question 100% of the time is? **"That sounds great."**

We are going to check for acceptance a few times throughout our ten step sales process. Do not skip this step! There is INSANE amount of power psychologically in those four words, *"How does that sound?"*

Checking for acceptance puts your prospects on what I refer to as the "**yes** train." The more you can get them to say yes or agree with you during the sales process, the harder it is for them to say no at the end. Think about that. I ask you eight questions throughout my sales process, and you answer yes or agree with me on all eight questions. When we get to the end, are you more likely to say yes or no?

Checking for acceptance also makes sure you are both on the same page. If you say something, and then immediately check for acceptance and they don't understand, then they have the opportunity to ask a question to clarify. Do not skip checking for acceptance. It will keep you in control of the process, it will put you and the prospect on the same page, and it will allow your prospect to climb aboard the *yes* train.

Steps 3 & 4: Probe and Support

Step 3 in the process is probing.

That's such a funny word. It sounds uncomfortable, but that is by design because, up until this point, everything has been all nice/nice warm and fuzzy with our prospect (who, if you haven't noticed, I named John, for no particular reason).

Let's recap.

We've built rapport. We've expressed John some gratitude. We shared our value statement with John. We checked for acceptance to make sure John is picking up everything we are putting down. In Step 3, we have to ask John a disturbing question.

Now, there are only a few different types of probing questions we can ask. Who? What? How? Why? You can pick one of them or all of them. It doesn't matter, as long as the question (or questions) you ask will get John to acknowledge that he has absolutely no clue what coverage he has, how he chose it, and why he even pays for it each month.

The questions sound like this: "John, tell me who your current agent is?" I like to throw him a softball first, although about a quarter of your prospects can't even answer that.

Then I ask, "What made you choose them?" Here is where you'll get, "Price," or, "My brother sent me there," or, "They were close to my house," something that offers no real value to the customer. I acknowledge John's response with, "That makes sense, John." Now, I ask the disturbing question. "Tell me, how did you go about choosing your current coverage?"

Here is when you get the silence over the phone or the blank stare in person. This will be followed by, "They gave it to me," or, "They matched what I had" or "I have full coverage." Again, whatever they say here will be something that offers John zero value.

Finally, the fourth question I ask is, "Well, what was it about that coverage that made you decide to go with such and such agency?" At this point, John has probably thrown in the towel and will admit he has no idea what he has or why he has it.

Now, we move to Step 4, which is support. Keep in mind, we are all humans, and as humans, we all need love and support, so now that John has admitted that he has no idea what he has or why he has it, we are going to give him our "Support Statement."

Mine sounds like this: *"John, we have dozens of people who call or stop by our agency each day wanting to do business here. Each time I ask those questions, the number one answer I get is, 'I don't know," so don't feel bad. You're not alone.*

However, that is a big problem because I'm guessing you spend a lot of your hard-earned money on your insurance each month. Shouldn't you know what you have and why you have it?"

Two things happened there.

1. I added a credibility statement to my support statement.
2. I ended by keeping John on the ***yes*** train.

What is a credibility statement? It's something that you say confidently and matter-of-factly which subconsciously allows the prospect to know that you are a big deal and somebody they should be doing business with.

I opened my support statement with, "Each day, we have dozens and dozens of people either calling or stopping by the agency wanting to do business with us." This covers FOMO as well, Fear of Missing Out. People will move faster to avoid loss than they will to realize a gain. "Wait? What? Everybody wants to do business here? Shoot, so do I!" Then, at the end, I stressed that John is spending a lot of his hard-earned money on insurance, so shouldn't he know what he's buying and why he's buying it? One hundred percent of your prospects will answer that question with yes and you will be thinking in your head, "CHOO CHOO"! I am keeping them on the ***yes*** train!"

Step 5: Setting the Agenda, Checking for Acceptance

We are approximately three to five minutes into the process and we have established trust. The prospect likes us because we've shown genuine interest in them. We've dropped a few reasons on them explaining why we are different and better than our competition. We've made sure they're still with us. We've disturbed them a bit, but then we supported them and lifted their spirits back up.

Now we are ready to set the agenda, to provide them with a road map as to how this process will work. Here is how we set the agenda at my agency. Pay attention for the additional credibility builder upfront.

"John, here at our agency we insure over 4,000 great people like you! Every single day, as sure as the sun comes up, we have at least one claim. Most days, we have numerous claims. "Now, we never know whose day it's going to be. It could be a friend of yours, somebody in your neighborhood, or somebody you have never met. However, we do know for certain, tomorrow, it will be somebody's turn in this community.

"Our promise is to make certain that, when your day comes to have a claim (and one day, it will), you are properly protected, because that's the exact reason you pay for insurance.

"Don't you agree?"

"We've been here for almost 10 years, now, and over the past decade, we've seen every single type of claim there is. They've ranged from basic glass repairs to, unfortunately, auto fatalities and everything in between. "What I'd like to do with the remainder of our time today is to first take you through a couple boring questions and then, share with you some actual claims stories we've seen, so you get a better understanding of how insurance works this way you can tell me which coverages are most important to you.

"How does that sound?"

Let's take a second to break that down.

The first thing I said is we insure over 4,000 great people like John here in our community. Again, that's a credibility builder. We are a big deal and a lot of people trust us. Next, every single day, we have claims. This tells John that (a) the risk out there is real, it happens all the time, and (b) we know what we are doing. Next, we don't know when you'll have your claim, but you will. When you do, we want to make sure you're properly protected. This goes back to knowing what you have and why you have it. Next, we've been here almost 10 years and we've seen it all (another credibility builder). Our resume includes a range of things from glass repair to fatality and everything in between.

(You can trust us; we have experience.) Where's the check for acceptance? This is us saying "You want to be properly protected when it's your turn to have a claim, right, John?" Yes? (CHOO CHOO!)

Then we continue with what John can expect: a couple boring questions and then a couple of real-life claims we've seen so he can better understand how insurance works. Add in another check for acceptance, "You cool with that, John? Oh, you are?" (CHOO CHOO.)

Step 6: More Rapport, Boring Questions, Detective Skills

The application you are completing is to ultimately get a rate on the auto insurance. However, now that you've read this book, you know you are an Opportunity Optimizer and you get paid to solve ALL your prospect's problems, not just the auto piece.

While you are going to use the auto application as a guide, what you're doing is turning yourself into a detective by asking super critical questions outside of the application, which will be important for you to know at the end of this process.

Keep in mind you are not selling anything during this total protection conversation. In fact, at my agency, we only have to sell two things during the sales process: the value of the face-to-face meeting and the importance of the referral.

During this part of the process, you'll be making handwritten notes on the side. Like a squirrel gathering nuts for the winter, you're going to stash this information away for later.

The very first question, which is on every application ever made, is "NAME." Obviously, we've been calling John by name throughout this process, so we know his, but this is where you ask, "John, I know you are a driver in the household, but are there any others?" If John says no, that's easy. However, if John says, "Yes, my wife, Mary, as well," then we follow up with, "Great! Now, when it comes to making decisions regarding your insurance plan, who makes those decisions, you, Mary, or both of you together?"

This is crucial information when we get to the end. Regardless of how John answers, it doesn't matter for now. You're still going to continue, but you'll want to squirrel that away. As you answer all the boring questions on the auto application, you continue to build rapport. Don't ask for occupations; find out where they work and how long they've been there. Don't ask if they are a homeowner or renter, ask the homeowners how long they've owned the home and what their future plans are for the home.

Ask both homeowners and renters what they own of value inside those four walls. Do they have any jewelry, firearms, art, computers, iPads, or collectables? Again, we're squirrelling this info away for now.

When you are entering the cars, ask about the lienholders. Who are they? How much do they still owe? What do they pay each month for car payment? Then, when you get to the part of the application where you select coverage that starts Step 7 of the process.

Steps 7-10

This is where the magic happens. You have built rapport, expressed gratitude, shared your value statement, asked probing questions, supported their responses, set the agenda, established trust and credibility, uncovered some initial opportunities and all throughout the process the prospect has agreed with you and answered YES to your questions at least five different times. Now you are finally ready to share the stories you created to properly explain exactly how insurance works. And Step seven of our sales process will allow you to share your stories in such a way that prospects will be telling you exactly how they want to be covered.

Once you master step seven, prospects will give you permission to quote numerous lines of insurance which properly protect them. This is the winning formula to truly help more people in more ways forever and create a multi-line insurance agency which will dominate your market year after year.

If you are **serious** about taking your agency's production to the next level you will want complete access to my Agency Optimization system as a **MASTERMIND member**.

Visit my website: www.agencyoptimization.com Here you will find everything I offer in my live seminars and to the Agents I personally coach. MASTERMIND members gain access to the "20 Must WIN Areas" training videos, over ten hours of impactful content including this game changing ten step, multi-line sales process. MASTERMINDS also gain access to my Toolkit with cheat sheets, extra trainings and numerous other valuable resources. Finally, this membership provides you and your team with daily virtual coaching from me every single day because true success is an everyday thing. Each morning I will push into your office virtually with a 5-10 minute training which will end with a call to action so your team can get to work implementing what they just learned immediately. Have a question about something you just learned? Ask it in our private MASTERMIND Facebook group and I will personally answer it for you!

There is **nothing** available to insurance agents today that can match the Agency Optimization MASTERMIND membership. This platform combines every training tool there is and the best part is, it never leaves you. You and your team will have complete access to all of the game changing content at your fingertips, right within your agency. Plus, you will receive new training content every single day and access to a group of like-minded individuals to learn, share and grow with.

Agency changing content, new daily trainings from one of the most sought after coaches in the industry, cheat sheets, tips, tricks, systems, processes and mindsets all in one place, for one membership and it's only pennies per day!

Practice, Practice, Practice

One of my favorite writers is Malcom Gladwell, who wrote one of my favorite books, *Outliers.* In that book, he proves to the world that nobody has ever reached the top of their field (any field, art, music, literature, business, sports, doesn't matter) until they put in a minimum of 10,000 hours of practice.

Here we were all excited you reached the end of this book, and now I tell you that you're 9,998 hours short of attaining greatness. Buzzkill!

However, we started this with a couple of promises:

1. We'd close the knowledge-action gap.
2. This wasn't a quick fix.
3. There are no shortcuts to success.

I am confident that everything you've learned will change you and improve you. However, don't lose sight of the grit and faith required from here. While you've reached the end of this book (almost), technically, you're only beginning. Remember, people fail because they cannot close the knowledge-action gap. You now have the knowledge you need to be happier, healthier, and to take your productivity to the next level. You will be a top 10% producer in this industry, but only if you take action. You need to take action by practicing. You need to put in your 10,000 hours, not all at once, but no results are ever attained all at once.

A guiding principle of continuous improvement is small daily actions will compound over time into massive results. You need to practice, role play and be accountable to yourself every single day. If you are unwilling to put in the work and practice every day, you should make a sign that says, "I quit learning and improving years ago," and put it on your desk. This way, people will know they should only expect mediocrity from you.

But you are here at the end, so that is not you. You understand the importance of repetition. You understand the concept of muscle memory, and you now know how to create and develop success habits.

Again, much of this is new and uncomfortable, but that's by design. You already know what to expect if you keep doing things the same way. Today, I want you to challenge yourself to try and try and keep trying. You need to understand we don't chase perfection, we chase continuous improvement. Understand, you will never blow a sale because of something you say. You will only blow sales opportunities with the things you don't say or by telling yourself you can't do something.

The only way you can guarantee failure is by not making a call, not following up, not building rapport, not expressing gratitude, not sharing your value statement, not showing them you're different, not telling your stories, not asking the disturbing questions, not checking for acceptance along the way, not keeping them on the *yes* train, not being prepared to overcome objections, not fighting to get in front of them, not presenting all of the options that will best protect them.

You have to trust the process. You have to trust and believe in yourself. You are one decision away from changing your sales career as an insurance producer. Don't be afraid to make that decision. Don't be afraid to answer this question: Are you willing to put in the work required to be one of the best in this industry?

If so, join us as an Agency Optimization MASTERMIND member today!

Chapter 9:
Earning More Referrals

There's a difference between earned and expected. You are not entitled to the names of people's friends and family. Throwing a $10 gift card at them doesn't make you worthy of those names either. Think of yourself. How protective are you of your inner circle? What makes you refer people to others? I encourage you to use our four-step process to earn more referrals at your agency.

Step one, is to be worthy. Create a unique, memorable, and valuable customer experience. Don't be Bruno from the jewelry store taking the path of least resistance and looking for a quick and easy sale. Instead, be John, the guy who makes others feel special, valuable, and takes the time to get to know them, understands their needs, and offers the best solution.

Step two, put their contacts right out in front of them. Make them get out their phones. Does your company offer an app they can download? Have them download it. Also, let them know how to reach you. Ask them to add your agency's phone number to their contacts.

Step three, ask them if you are worthy. Have them share with you how they felt about their experience at your agency. Create a short, clean, one-page customer satisfaction survey. On it, ask simple questions such as cleanliness of grounds, temperature of office, the aroma. Were they greeted professionally? Were they offered a snack or beverage? Did their insurance professional help them understand how policies work? Did they share stories about how insurance protection works? Were they offered solutions to all their needs? Would they recommend us to their friends and family? These can be yes or no questions or rate on a scale of one to five or one to 10. It's your survey. Ask whatever you'd like, but make sure it ends with asking if they would recommend you to friends and family.

The remainder of the page contains spaces asking them for the names, relationships, and phone numbers of the friends and family they said they'd recommend. Remember, this comes right after you asked them to enter your agency phone number into their contacts, so their phones are already out.

The key to this satisfaction survey is to do two things: A) explain this is how you earn a living, 100% of your business comes from great people like them sharing thoughts, feedback, and names of other great people they know; and B) after you sell yourself and the importance of the survey, you have to leave the room so they are comfortable, and then you don't step back into that room until they are done.

Step four, hopefully, when you come back into the room, there are names on that paper. If so, have a separate piece of paper prepared with the following words on it. "I changed my insurance over to the Scott Grates Agency. They were awesome to work with and I highly recommend you give them an opportunity to look at your insurance, too. I shared your number and asked him to give you a call, but if you want to call Scott sooner, here is his information." Then, have your business card displayed below that. While you finish up the paperwork, kindly ask your customer if they would take a picture of that paper and text it to the names on the recommended list. This way, they aren't caught off guard when you call, and they have your information in advance. This is what I refer to as a "warm introduction" in our highly digital world.

Chapter 10:
Insurance Agency Optimization Can Guide You to Market Domination

You are an insurance agent. That's probably not what you dreamed of being as a child. However, your story can have a happy ending because this is a pretty amazing place to be!

Successful Agents enjoy a healthy work/life balance. They manage, lead, motivate, and inspire those who work for them every single day. They protect their customers with more products, in more ways, so when the unexpected happens, they are prepared and can recover quickly.

Insurance Agents donate their time and financial resources back into the communities they serve.

The Agents who build a career around doing the right thing, for the right person, 100% of the time leave a legacy behind them which continues to help others long after they are gone.

There are over 100,000 licensed insurance producers on the planet. This means there are over one million thoughts, ideas, tips, tricks, systems, processes, and best practices being used sporadically each day around the globe.

Insurance Agency Optimization was written with the intent to take the common denominator principles from those millions of ideas and condense them into one place. Author Scott Grates built his insurance agency from the ground up. Scott has spent his entire career leading, coaching, and training others to take their sales production to the next level. In 2019, Scott created the Agency Optimization MASTERMIND group, which is an online insurance training website for Agents and Team Members who have a true passion for continuous improvement.

With a focus on overall health, happiness, and increased productivity, *Insurance Agency Optimization* serves as a guide to the Agents who desire:

- A winning office culture.
- A team who carries out the Agency mission with passion and purpose.

- An efficient agency strategy with a focus on only the essentials while optimizing every opportunity.
- A daily plan for dominance backed by proper preparation and personal accountability.
- A team of individuals, who think bigger, refuse to quit, and remain positive while experiencing the inevitable setbacks.
- A proven sales process which allows customers and prospects to share all their needs and concerns.
- Simple and repeatable word tracks that will allow your producers to write new business, regardless of rate, and protect more customers beyond their auto policy.

Cut through the clutter and stand above the competition by creating a unique and memorable customer experience. Earn more referrals than ever before because, frankly, now you are worthy of them!

Here's How The Agency Optimization MASTERMIND Membership Can Guide You to Market Domination

While this *Insurance Agency Optimization* book is a great starting point, it certainly isn't the end. The Agency Optimization MASTERMIND membership was designed as a one stop shop online training and development site so it could remain up to date within an ever-changing insurance industry. It is Scott's mission to deliver his MASTERMIND members daily content, tie them into a community of like-minded individuals, and promote personal accountability around continuous improvement. Everybody is at a different point in their agency career and has different goals.

However, there are common denominators to success regardless of industry. After a decade of running one of the top producing multi-line insurance agencies in America, Scott has identified 20 MUST WIN AREAS for all insurance agency owners to dominate in.

They are:

1. Building your Agency Foundation (out of bricks)
2. Understanding the Insurance industry & your Compensation
3. Recruiting, hiring, onboarding & training quality Team Members
4. Health, Happiness, Productivity
5. Mission, Passion, Purpose & Why
6. Create a Championship Office Culture
7. Opportunity Optimization
8. Creating a Unique Customer Experience
9. Becoming More Efficient with your time
10. MINDSET is EVERYTHING
11. Preparing your team for sales
12. The Sales Process (Steps 1-6)
13. The Power of Story in Sales (step 7)
14. The Sales Process (steps 8-10)
15. The IFR process

16. Become a Referral Rock Star

17. Retention Strategies

18. Quotes for a Cause

19. Life, Health & Bank Sales Made Easy

20. Grass Roots Marketing

Obviously clicking on ALL cylinders in each of these 20 areas at once is NOT easy. You may have gaps or weaknesses in some of these areas at the moment. However, fear not! Your MASTERMIND membership will provide you with a roadmap for success in each of those 20 MUST WIN AREAS, keep you motivated and hold you accountable ALL 250+ workdays each and every year!

Scott also shares with his members the 7 most common traps insurance agencies fall into and how to avoid them.

Do what the top 10% in the insurance industry do...TAKE ACTION. Become a MASTERMIND member TODAY!

www.agencyoptimization.com

Made in the USA
Coppell, TX
17 January 2020